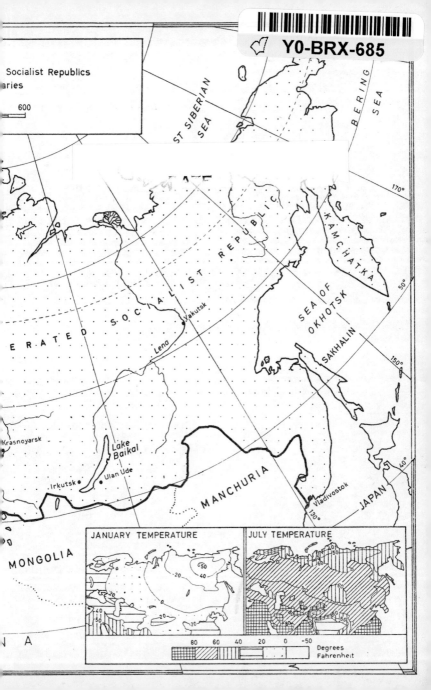

*Oxford University Press, Amen House, London E.C.4*

GLASGOW   NEW YORK   TORONTO   MELBOURNE   WELLINGTON
BOMBAY   CALCUTTA   MADRAS   KARACHI   LAHORE   DACCA
CAPE TOWN   SALISBURY   NAIROBI   IBADAN   ACCRA
KUALA LUMPUR   HONG KONG

© *Oxford University Press,* 1963

PRINTED   IN   GREAT   BRITAIN   BY
NORTHUMBERLAND PRESS LIMITED
GATESHEAD   ON   TYNE

THE MODERN WORLD
GENERAL EDITOR: C. H. C. BLOUNT

# THE U.S.S.R.

BY

WRIGHT MILLER

OXFORD UNIVERSITY PRESS
1963

# CONTENTS

# LIST OF PLATES

*Cover:* Statue of Lenin by People's Artist Merkurov installed in the Hall of Arts of the Central Lenin Museum, Moscow

Illustrations are reproduced by courtesy of The Society for Cultural Relations with the U.S.S.R.: the cover photograph and Plates 2, 4a, 6a, 7a; John Hillelson Agency Ltd.: Plate 1; John Massey Stewart: Plates 3a, 3b, 3c, 3d, 4b, 5a, 5b, 6b, 8; Novosti Press Agency (A.P.N.): Plate 7b; *Radio Times* Hulton Picture Library: Plate 7c.

# I

## THE COUNTRY AND THE PEOPLE

WHEN PEOPLE START listening to classical music their first enthusiasm is nearly always for Tchaikovsky; he seems able most easily to rise to the heights or plunge into the depths of all human emotions. And when one first reads great novels it is not long before one finds, as almost everyone else has done before, that the greatest, the most natural, of all novelists is Tolstoy. 'Life seems more like life', people say, in *Anna Karenina* and *War and Peace* than they had ever thought possible. When the characters show their feelings one is convinced that these are their real feelings and not something whipped up for the occasion, nor a cover for something else. The best-drawn characters seem to be so remarkably like ourselves, especially when they feel shy or inadequate, although they don't seem to be so embarrassed about shyness or inadequacy as we would be.

Tolstoy's most famous characters, such as Kitty and Levin in *Anna Karenina* or Pierre in *War and Peace*, were aristocrats, yet in spite of all the changes made by the Russian Revolution they are still typical of what is best in the people of Soviet Russia. Tolstoy is revered and admired there today for his Russian sincerity and directness, and there are still no better introductions to the 'feel' of the Russian people than writers such as Tolstoy and Tchehov, and composers such as Tchaikovsky and Borodin.

Russians do not have, and have never had, the formal, classical characteristics of such nations as the French; they missed the classical Latin influence entirely, both

5

the influence of ancient Rome and that of the Roman Catholic Church, and this is one of the more important things to note about them. In personal relations they appear natural and straightforward in rather the way that English people like; they are less inclined than we are to cover up feelings with a joke (though they have a great sense of humour); and also, because they like feelings to be genuine, they are less inclined to sentimentality than we are.

Russian sincerity has its defects, of course. A Russian of weak or bad character can be extremely boring, to say the least, and because Russians are so fond of behaving, on the whole, in the way that they feel, Western visitors often find them lacking in self-discipline. They are inclined, if left to themselves, to alternate between huge bouts of energy and periods of procrastination and idleness. They can put up with dreary monotony for long periods and then break out into abandoned enjoyment like the dances in *Prince Igor* or the fair scenes of *Petrouchka*. This does not work so badly as one might think, because most Russians behave in the same sort of way, and also because they have a remarkable sort of feeling among themselves, as though they all belonged to the same vast family; they can quarrel as people in families do, but they still remain within the family circle.

This family feeling makes for a great sense of equality between Russians—not a political but a personal, mostly unconscious, sort of equality. They are not brought up to assert their individualities in the way that people are in England or America or France. This was true before the Revolution and it is still true. Young children are not much disciplined—all Russians are very tolerant with children—and this does not create chaos because they are all being brought up in the same way; it seems to help Russians to a more natural self-confidence as they grow

6

up. If one were to join a Russian school one would find that it is often one's own schoolfellows who press one not to fall behind in lessons, while on the other hand if a pupil is singled out by the teacher for praise or blame, he or she does not seem set apart in the same way as in an English classroom. The same sort of feeling carries on into adult life, and has been much exploited by the Soviet authorities in distributing the many kinds of public rewards for the best workers and public shame for the worst. Russian egalitarianism also means a certain fundamental equality between the sexes as human beings, although most of the dirty and heavy work is done by women, and men rarely help in the home. It was not difficult for the Soviet Government to bring in equality of men and women before the law, and equal pay for both sexes, and to stop peasants beating their wives. The equality means that it is regarded as natural for a young man to strike up acquaintance with a girl, and if the girl doesn't want him he can usually take no for an answer. Also—strange custom for us from Western countries—if a girl wants to strike up acquaintance with a young man she can do so without being thought forward.

To describe Russians in such a general way is bound, of course, to give a rather ideal impression. There are still peasants who beat their wives, there are some young men whose approaches a girl may need a brother's help to get rid of, and there is a good deal of theft and even burglary and robbery with violence. This is rarely reported in Soviet papers, unless there has been such a wave of it that the Government wants to publicize the heavy sentences which have been imposed. There is a good deal of drunkenness in spite of the campaign against drink, and there are other kinds of crime, specially induced by the Soviet system of organization, which will be mentioned in Chapter 3.

7

After many long visits to Soviet Russia it seems to me that in order to try to answer the simple question—'What's Russia like?', one must begin with the people. The people were there before the system, and though they have been a good deal changed by it, they have also helped to condition the system. It is particularly important for English visitors to begin in this way, because English and Russians usually get on very well together if they can somehow cross the barrier of language. This barrier means more than in many other countries, because one can so easily get a false impression of the Russians as a dull, unsmiling people, with off-hand or even rude manners on the surface. But this is largely the result of their relaxed 'family' way of not bothering too much about each other. As soon as one can exchange a few words with them or establish the rudiments of a personal relationship, the genuineness of the average Russian personality comes most pleasantly to the surface.

Another reason for beginning with the people is that Russia is a country whose appearance conveys much less than the average traveller would like. One cannot pick up the 'flavour' of Russia in the easy way that one can absorb the 'flavour' of Paris or Florence or Amsterdam while knowing only a few words of French, Italian, or Dutch.

Russians in general have always been poor, and to this day, in spite of great improvements, their standard of living is well behind our own. Over the centuries there were very few prosperous merchants or farmers to build up comfortable little towns such as our own Broadway, Lewes, Stratford-on-Avon, or Culross. Most Russians have until recently been peasants (and for several centuries before 1861 serfs); they have lived, as most Russian country people do today, in one-room, wooden huts, and the typical Russian village still consists of a broad, muddy

8

track, anything up to fifty yards wide, with the little huts on each side, spaced far apart so that if one catches fire it does not set light to the rest. The track has to be broad, so that when ruts have been ploughed too deep by the wheels of the little wooden carts or the churning tractors, another set of ruts can be started. There is no road surface, only bare earth and weeds, and when you come to a shallow stream or lake, if the bottom is firm enough you simply go splashing through.

The greater part of the U.S.S.R. is dotted with lakes and ponds, marshes and pools, rivers and cut-offs, and these are what one sees most of from a plane. The straggling villages can be picked out easily, but they don't come very often, and most of Russia, whether in the forest belt or the steppe land, is as thinly inhabited as the north of Scotland—much more thinly in the North of the U.S.S.R. or over most of Asia. Only in the industrial areas of the Ukraine, the Urals, and West Siberia, and around Moscow and Leningrad, is there a density of population such as we know. The railways seem none too frequent, and the rarest sight of all is a long-distance metalled road. Elsewhere the earth tracks have to serve.

On the ground one finds that Russia on the whole is not monotonously dead flat; the monotony comes rather from the repetition of little rises and ravines, forests and rivers. After a time one longs for something as definite as the Pennines, but over most of Russia it is not to be had. There is a wonderful sense of space and to spare; the country seems freer and wilder than anything in England, there are no hedges or walls between the fields of corn, potatoes, flax, sugarbeet, or sunflowers, and in the forests there are still wolves and bears and lynxes not far from Moscow. If you live in a Soviet city and go out into the country at weekends you probably go for a bathe in a lake or river, and for country food; baskets of wild strawberries and

9

raspberries are to be had for the picking, mushrooms later in the season, and from the peasants you buy honey. The Russians are great beekeepers, and they eat more honey per head than any nation in the world.

That is for the summer, and over most of the U.S.S.R. the summer is hotter and drier than in England. Even in Archangel the temperature can reach 80° F. But the summer is short, and packed with furious hard work for the peasants, who must get ploughing, sowing, haymaking, and reaping all done between April and September. At the end of September it is already cold, and then the miserable period of autumn rain begins, when a great deal of the country is bogged down for a few weeks and no vehicles can stir. The frost comes as a relief, and the people are as delighted with the first crisp snow as though spring had come. But even Russians find the winter far too long; in Moscow there can be seven months of frost and snow in a bad year, and at least four months in a good one. In the middle of winter the burning cold is something of which we have no idea in Britain. You do not shiver, you do not get colds or chilblains, because the weather is so dry; you shrivel and shrink from the cold, or else you go out as the Russians do, in a very thick winter coat, fur cap, proper boots, and all your underclothes—for without all these you would die—and you brave and fight the cold, with little icicles forming on your hair and nose. It is wonderful exercise to be outside for even half an hour, and nowadays millions of Russians of all ages go out on Sunday in light windproof clothes and spend the short winter day on skis.

But whether inside the stuffy little peasant huts or the centrally-heated flats, winter slows everything down and has to be fought. Windows must be double and sealed round the edges, doors must be double or treble, and even potatoes have to travel in heated trains. The Russian winter is the oldest thing in Russian history, and with every modern device, it has still to be endured. The spring comes late and suddenly, in April or early May, with the spring flowers in a wild rush—catkins and fruit blossom and lilac all over in a few weeks. The thaw makes another spell of 'roadlessness', as the Russians call it, and then the hot summer's toil begins again.

In Soviet cities there is a good deal of the same sense of space as in the country. The dingy streets of two-storey, nineteenth century stucco stretch interminably, and the new blocks of flats and theatres and public buildings are built on broad avenues and huge squares which quite dwarf human beings. That was usually the way in Tsarist Russia too. Leningrad (the old St. Petersburg) is one of the most beautiful cities in the world, but it covers huge spaces on which a walking visitor feels that he can make little impression. The Tsars, the Church, and some of the noblemen were the only source of grand building, and some of their palaces and monasteries are as grand as anything in Western Europe. But everyone else necessarily lived on a mean scale. And today the imposing buildings are provided by the government; there is little which shows the mark of one man's personality, except the shacks and modest wooden summer houses (dachas) which are scattered round the cities.

The history of the Russian people is for the next chapter; for introduction I wanted to sketch in the background—the inescapable winter, the delirious spring and short summer, the lavishness of space, and the general feeling that impressive, or grand, or new things must come from the central authority, whether Tsarist or Soviet, rather than from the enterprise of individuals.

This is not to say that creative individuals do not receive their due—but they receive it as artists, inventors, or 'heroes of Socialist labour', not as the creators of great enterprises or cities. Even the top Soviet leaders, whose portraits weary the tourist with repetition, are held up for admiration as governors, and not because they have personally organized great works or institutions.

The line of great Russians does not stretch so far back into the past as the line of great Englishmen or Frenchmen. There are comparatively few great names until the end of the eighteenth century. Pushkin, the greatest and most Russian of all Russian writers, died only in 1837; the great novelists and composers belong to the nineteenth and twentieth centuries, and there are people still alive who knew Tolstoy, Tchehov, or Tchaikovsky. The great Russian scientists belong to the same period—the chemist Mendeleef, who drew up the table of atomic weights (1834-1907); Lobachevsky, the inventor of non-Euclidean geometry (1793-1856); Dokuchaev, the founder of soil science (1846-1903); Yablochkoff (1847-94), who invented the electric lamp before Edison; and others. Russians are very conscious that the greatness of their country is comparatively recent; this accounts partly for the *naïveté* which they often show in talking about Russian achievements.

It would be of great interest to discuss also the effect of Russian climate and geography on the Russian character. There is only room here to remark that these effects cannot be taken as automatic; for example, the Canadians, the Americans of the northern Mid-West, and their Red Indian predecessors have all had to endure winters even colder than any in European Russia, but their reactions to their climate have been different from those of the Russians. The great size of Russia and its position as what geographers call an 'inner country' have made the people feel set in their own world and suspicious of foreigners, who have indeed generally come as invaders across their open frontiers; yet even so, if Russia had had an enlightened government and some popular education earlier in her history, the attitude to foreigners might have been different. Soviet Russia is in a state of transition, learning much from abroad but disinclined to admit the fact; the people as well as the government are touchy about their backwardness, and they expect for their industrial and scientific achievements a more open and unqualified appreciation than people from Western countries are usually able to give. Russians can lose their natural sincerity where their country or their group is concerned, and many of them are ready to mistake a project for a reality. They are too proud and masculine, also, to speak readily of their appalling sufferings during the last war, but they expect foreigners to bear these constantly in mind. Western visitors, on the other hand, are often unable to understand the transitional state in which the U.S.S.R. finds itself. The *sputniks* and great electric schemes do not imply a similar level in all kinds of technology or organization; but on the other hand the shortages of so many things which we take for granted, the frequent slatternliness, backwardness, and lack of order —all easily observed by the tourist—these do not necessarily imply inefficiency in the great industrial enterprises which are usually kept away from his view. Around Russian cities the peasants live in one-room huts with few household goods, but they nearly all sport TV aerials; the contrast might be taken as a symbol of the intermediate state of Soviet Russia today.

Many readers will by now be objecting that the Soviet Union is a country of many nationalities, and that I have been writing exclusively about Russians. The U.S.S.R. is indeed described as a federation of fifteen republics, but fourteen of these take up only 25 per cent of the area. The fifteenth, the Russian Soviet Federated Socialist Republic (R.S.F.S.R.), occupies three-quarters of the country, including the whole of Siberia, and it includes 56 per cent. of the population. Not all of these are Russians, but there are large numbers of Russians in all the republics. The Communist Revolution was made mainly by Russians in the cities of European Russia, its direction has stayed tightly concentrated in Moscow, and the Russian element is overwhelmingly predominant in 'the Soviet personality'.

It is said that 115 languages are taught in Soviet schools —some of them languages spoken by only a few thousand people, who had no alphabet until the Soviet period. But every Soviet child, whatever its native language, also learns Russian from the age of seven, and by the age of fourteen is expected to speak it fairly well. Russian is the dominant language of the U.S.S.R., and it might be difficult to carry on government if this were not so.

It is notable that the fourteen non-Russian Republics are all situated on the periphery; they have either a frontier with a foreign country or a seaboard. There are other large units of population, such as the Tartars, speaking their own language and having their own culture, who live well away from the frontier and are included within one of the Federated Republics as Autonomous Soviet Socialist Republics or National Areas, with something of the status that Wales has within the United Kingdom. The superior status of the Federated Republics does not confer much more autonomy; their budgets are incorporated in the All-Union budget, and though their constitutions include a clause allowing for the possibility of secession, this can hardly be regarded as more than a dead letter. Yet the status may give some satisfaction to national pride and may, for example, lead 1.4 million Tadjiks on the Afghan border to be less anxious to break away and join their fellow Tadjiks in Afghanistan; on the contrary, there may be a hope that the Afghan Tadjiks could be induced to come over and increase the Tadjik S.F.S.R. (The Soviet Tadjiks are far fewer in number than the Tartars, who amount to five million but do not have Federal-Republican status. Located as they are around their capital Kazan, in the heart of the U.S.S.R., they are not in a position to influence external affairs much.)

To get Soviet nationalities into perspective the most practical thing is to arrange them in groups, not according to their administrative status but roughly according to the kind of civilization they have. The following figures are those of the 1959 census, when the total population was returned as 208.8 millions; the classification is my own.

| | |
|---|---|
| (1) Russian and near-Russian peoples (Russians, Ukrainians, Belorussians, and a few others). | 164.6 millions |
| (2) Peoples who enjoyed better conditions, on the whole, before they came under Soviet domination (Estonians, Latvians, Lithuanians). | 4.66 millions |
| (3) Peoples of older civilizations than the Russians (Armenians and Georgians). | 5.45 millions |
| (4) Peoples of old Muslim civilization, materially and socially often backward but far from primitive (Uzbeks, etc.). | 16.3 millions |
| (5) Other peoples—mainly small units scattered over the whole country, ranging from nomadic hunters to Finns, Poles, and Moldavians who enjoyed a fair standard on the western border before they were incorporated. | 17.79 millions |

*1. Russian and near-Russian peoples:* Of these the Russians alone number 114.6 millions, and there are 37 million Ukrainians and 7.8 million Belorussians who differ from them, in their ways, about as much as the Scots differ from the English. The Ukrainian and Belorussian languages, which diverged from Russian only a few centuries ago, are still about as close to Russian as the dialect of Burns is to Standard English. The Ukrainians are more lively, independent, and individualistic than the Russians; there was never much serfdom in the Ukraine, and the land was tilled by individual farmers, while the Russians from time immemorial have farmed on a community basis. The Ukraine has been undergoing industrialization since the eighteenth century, and the Russian and Ukrainian peoples have been a good deal mixed up together, but old traditions, and the absorption of Ukrainian districts which were under Poland, have left a residual feeling of Ukrainian nationalism which is sometimes embarrassing to the Soviet Government. The Belorussians are a hardy people who have made a living from rather poor land; in speech and ways they differ even less from the Russians than Ukrainians do. It is notable that at the United Nations the U.S.S.R. has representatives of the whole country and of the Ukrainian and Belorussian Republics, but not of any other Republic.

In this near-Russian group one should also include the 2.3 million Jews of the U.S.S.R., who live mostly in the Russian and Ukrainian Republics. Most of the Soviet Jews were killed by the Nazis. A great many of those who remain are completely assimilated to Russian or Ukrainian ways and would be only too glad to get rid of the entry 'Jew' on their identity papers, since there is a good deal of discrimination against them. They no longer suffer physical persecution as they did under the Tsars, but there is much anti-Jewish feeling, and it is far from easy for Jews to preserve their language and religion. The Russian-born correspondent Maurice Hindus on his visit in 1960 thought that anti-semitism had increased since the nineteen-thirties.

It is fair also to include with near-Russian peoples a few groups such as the Mordvins—originally connected with the Finns—who have been in contact with Russians for so long that they are almost as assimilated as the Welsh are in Britain.

2. *Peoples who have enjoyed better conditions:* These are the Estonians, Latvians, and Lithuanians—peoples of the three Baltic Republics who had their independence (in recent centuries) only between the two World Wars, but had long been affected by Swedish, Finnish, or German as well as Russian or Polish influences. The Estonian language is close to Finnish; the Latvian and Lithuanian languages form the very old Baltic family of Aryan languages. Russians who visit these republics today are often delighted with the cleanliness, good order, and good design which prevail, particularly in Estonia and Latvia. (Lithuania was always rather worse off.) The two republics contribute a quite disproportionate amount of the clean Scandinavian type of design which is beginning very slowly (but with official encouragement) to compete with the heavy Victorian types of furniture, fabrics, china and glass which are usual in Russia. Many Estonians and Latvians are probably among the least satisfied of Soviet citizens; Lithuanians may also suffer because they are Catholics.

3. *Peoples of older civilization than the Russians:* These are the Armenians and Georgians, who were Christianized early in the fourth century. Georgia and Armenia are hot, mountainous, wine-growing countries, and foreigners often find their peoples 'more European than Russians seem to be', rather like Italians or Greeks. They are lively, hot-blooded, sallow-skinned peoples who show their passions more readily than Russians do and are proud of

their ancient cultures. Georgians often rather look down on Russians, and they set up a socialist republic of their own for some years after the Revolution. Georgia and Armenia were not annexed to Russia until the period 1800-30, but they had not always been independent before, and the Armenians had suffered cruel massacres under the Turks. Both peoples seem to have come to reasonable terms with the Russians, and they are left to run their affairs with a much smaller admixture of Russian personnel than is usual in other Republics. The Armenians show themselves to be as sharp-witted as Armenians elsewhere, and one of them, the ingenious Mikoyan, has been a member of the leading group in the Kremlin since the early days, surviving all purges and changes of policy. Both Georgia and Armenia have a literature which is centuries old, and there is a school of modern Armenian painters whose work is freer and more impressionistic than the work of most Soviet Russian artists. Stalin came from Georgia, but it would be very misleading to take that paranoiac dictator as typical of Georgians in general; they are traditionally inclined to nurse insults and cultivate revenge, but they also have a warm capacity for friendship which Stalin lacked entirely.

4. *Peoples of Muslim culture:* For about two thousand years Central Asia was the source from which hordes of horsemen descended at intervals to pillage and occupy the richer, flatter lands to the west, south, and east. The Mongols who invaded China in the thirteenth century, and the Moguls who conquered India in the sixteenth, were near relations of the Tartars who held down Russia for 300 years, and the Turks who sacked Constantinople in 1453 and ruled the Balkans for four and a half centuries. The home of these 'Turkic' peoples became known as Turkestan—in recent times divided between Russia, China, and Afghanistan.

18

The principal Muslim communities of the U.S.S.R. belong to these Turkic peoples (except for the Tadjiks, who are near-Persians). They include the 5 million Tartars, whose territory was absorbed long ago (the dancer Nureyev is one of them); the 2.9 million Azerbaidjanis, whose capital is the oil city of Baku on the Caspian, and who have been under Russian domination since 1828; and the 6 million Uzbeks and 1 million Turkmen, in the fertile valleys and oases of such centres as Tashkent, Bokhara, and Samarkand, who were only conquered during 1864-85. Also Turkic, and Muslim at least in name, are the 3.6 million Kazakhs, the 1 million Kirghiz, and the 1 million Bashkirs, but I have included them in the next group because they were until recently mostly nomads. The Uzbeks, Tartars, Azerbaidjanis, and Turkmen, on the other hand, have ancient cultures of their own and are sufficiently Muslim to have put up a good deal of resistance to Soviet emancipation of their women and other innovations. All these peoples speak languages fairly close to Turkish, and they have some tradition of the time when Turkic peoples ruled over vast areas of South-West Asia and Eastern Europe. The Soviet Government is vigilant to suppress manifestations of Tartar, Uzbek, or other nationalism, and still more any hint of a ' pan-Turanian union ' which sometimes filters through from a minority movement in Turkey. There is no doubt, however, that the Muslim communities are materially and socially better off than they used to be, though not yet, as a rule, so well off as the Russians. There is reciprocal bad feeling between, for instance, Uzbeks and Russians, but it is probably less than it was. The Uzbeks and Turkmen are the great cotton-growers of the U.S.S.R., the Azerbaidjanis produce grain, vegetables, fruit, and wine, or work in the oil industry, and all these Republics have some modern manufactures as well.

*5. Other peoples:* Apart from Finns, Poles, and Mold-
avians, these are mostly primitive peoples such as the
Kazakhs, whose huge semi-desert republic is being developed mainly by Russians; a number of very small nationalities isolated in the valleys of the Caucasus, with traditions of their own such as the blood feud; gypsies to the
number of 250,000; and small scattered groups of hunters,
reindeer herders, and fishermen in Siberia, including, on
the Bering Straits, a thousand or so genuine Eskimos.

The Soviet Government rightly claims credit for trying
to put its hundred or so nationalities on the same footing,
where in Tsarist times all were regarded as inferior to the
Russians. All have the full use of their own language
(though they must also learn Russian) and they have,
within the universal limits of Soviet censorship, their own
literature, music, dancing, and other arts, and sometimes
national dress. Russian literature is translated into the
other languages, and the literatures of these languages are
translated into Russian and sometimes into other minority
languages as well. So much is to be seen, in Moscow and
Leningrad, of the arts of the minorities that there one
can feel they are getting more than their share of repre-
sentation.

In political and social life, however, the picture is extremely different. Lesser peoples may retain their national
ways only where these do not conflict with the Soviet
system, and savage punishment fell on the Chechens, the
Ossetians, Crimean Tartars, and others who were accused
of disloyalty to the Soviet state. During the later years of
Stalin they were deported *en masse* from their homelands
in the Caucasus to inhospitable parts of Siberia or Asiatic
Russia. Under Khrushchev some of them, but not all,
have been allowed to return. The administration of the
minority nationalities is predominantly Russian, especially in Baltic or Asiatic republics or anywhere where resis-

tance still smoulders; Armenia and Georgia are exceptional in having republican affairs largely in native hands.

Four-fifths of the population may be counted as Russians or near-Russians; as for the multifarious social and political traditions of the other fifth, they contribute no more to the general Soviet way of life and Soviet 'image' than Highland Gaelic traditions have contributed to the English way of life. The influence is all the other way, in most republics. Russian attitudes, habits, and traditions, modified by Soviet ideology, are dominant, and their domination is going to increase in most parts of the U.S.S.R. The Soviet Union is much more an assimilating state than a multi-national state like Switzerland or Belgium. It is Russian ways which take over where blood feuds, bride purchase, subjection of women, ancestor-worship, nature-worship, etc., are suppressed. The Communist machine is a very powerful one in such respects as well as in imposing political and economic dictatorship, and it is Russian Communists who have made it so.

The rest of this book will deal almost exclusively with Russian/Soviet administration, ideas, and ways of life.

Soviet Communism is the system imposed from 1917 onwards, by leaders who were mostly Russians, on the Russian people with their own ancient characteristics and inheritance. This inheritance has helped to make Soviet Communism what it is in practice, and the blend of the two, exploiting the country's great natural resources, has made the U.S.S.R. into the second greatest industrial and military power in the world today.

Communism as a policy is founded largely on the doctrines of Karl Marx (1818-83), a German who lived the latter part of his life as a refugee in England and who had very little to do with Russia. Marx was not by any means the first socialist, but he used the often vague or abused word 'socialism' in a precise sense in which it is still used by most economists and political theorists, whether they are Marxists or not. He used it to mean a state of society in which the means of production and distribution are publicly owned, and no one receives any income (apart from pensions, etc.) except for work which he has done, and in accordance with the value of that work. Any rent, interest, or profit from the work of other people would be received by the state alone, and this, with some exceptions, is what happens in the U.S.S.R. The intention of such a socialist economic system is, of course, to provide a more just society. Marxists, however, condemn those socialists who strive for a just society through political, religious, or cultural reforms as merely 'Utopian'.

Out of his own theories and the work of many economists and philosophers Marx created a body of doctrine, known ever since as Marxism, which claims to explain almost everything in history, economics, and politics. The essence of the doctrine is the 'Economic Interpretation of History', or as Marxists call it, the 'Materialist Interpretation of History'. According to this theory it is always economic conditions which determine the course of history, while the political, social, religious, or cultural institutions and characteristics of a period are formed by the economic conditions. It was indeed useful in Marx's day to call attention to the fundamental importance of economic conditions, which had till then been mostly overlooked. Marx's view was a good deal more in accordance with the facts of history than some popular theories of long standing, such as 'the inevitability of progress', or the view that history is determined almost entirely by 'great men'. It was of great importance, for instance, to point out how far the rise of the English Parliament in the seventeenth century meant in fact the rise of the merchant or bourgeois class, or how far the growth of Puritanism and of Capitalism are connected, or how the well-known characteristics of Dutch seventeenth century painters were due to the fact that they had no clients but the merchant class, and it was for their houses that the painters had to produce sober portraits and representations of comfortable domestic interiors.

Today no reputable historian would deny such connections as these, and a great deal of excellent research has pursued the economic influences in history at some depth and in much detail. Most of this has been done by historians who were not Marxists, but for the first impulse to study the significance of economic factors we are all indebted to Marx.

Marx mostly studied and wrote about the era of modern capitalist society in which he lived. (His great work is simply called *Capital*.) He maintained that the condition of the industrial workers—then poor indeed—could not be improved so long as industry was organized for the private profit of its owners. The workers ('proletariat') would become more and more miserable as the capitalists squeezed more and more profit out of their labour, until by virtue of its 'inner contradictions' the whole capitalist system would be destroyed by the revolution of the workers, who would take power into their own hands. It was not difficult to hold this view in the industrial misery of Marx's day, but Marx did not foresee how capitalists might prefer to offer bribes rather than threats, so that workers in advanced countries such as America or Britain might become relatively more prosperous under a system still capitalist. Still less did he foresee how state (i.e. socialist) control would spread in countries with parliamentary government so as to produce a 'mixed' system such as now exists in Britain, the Scandinavian countries, or Israel.

Marx had little to say about the conditions which could make a workers' revolution successful in a predominantly peasant country such as Russia; he expected the Revolution to break out in one of the Western countries, and was actively involved in organizing some of the early workers' movements. Unfortunately he had a mania for making his theory into a universal one which would fit the whole of history, and he alleged that all great revolutionary changes consisted in fact of the working of 'inner contradictions' in an economic system which destroyed the power of the economically dominant class and replaced it by another.

Lenin trained himself in the doctrines of Marxism; he believed that improvement could only come through the revolutionary seizure of power by the workers, and few in number though the industrial workers were in Russia, he was able, through favourable historical accidents, to succeed. Lenin added to Marxist doctrine the principle that the workers could only be led to success by a small, highly disciplined and organized party—the Communist Party. (He originally believed that Russia must first pass through some kind of 'bourgeois parliamentary democracy' before she could become socialist.)

Stalin and his associates made the state a ruthless organ of dictatorship, in the name of the 'dictatorship of the proletariat', by which Marx had simply meant that when the workers had seized power they should see to it that the capitalists did not regain any of their former property or power.

The Stalinist dictatorship, though it brought about some very desirable progress, inevitably meant that the leadership must come to despise the people, as individuals, whom they were so ruthlessly driving 'for their own good'. It is from this position that Mr. Khrushchev and the more enlightened Soviet leaders are trying to extricate themselves today. This is not easy for them, because they were deeply involved in the Stalinist régime; if they had tried to modify it they might have lost their lives as other leaders did.

It should be noted that Communists, whether in the U.S.S.R. or elsewhere, use the terms 'Socialism' and 'Communism' in a sense which others do not. They preserve the terminology of Marx, by which a socialist society means one where men are rewarded according to the value of their work, while a communist society is one which is so prosperous that men simply draw from the common stock according to their needs. Thus the U.S.S.R. is regarded as still in the first stage, since there are great shortages and great differences of income; 'Communist society' is still the goal. 'Worker' for Communists has two meanings, which can be confusing when they are talking about foreign countries: one is the original Marxist meaning of the industrial workers—the class destined to make the Revolution; the other meaning covers everyone who is not a capitalist or an employer. Thus all Soviet citizens, from top ballerinas downwards, may be described as workers. It is quite common in the U.S.S.R. to speak of peasants, (industrial) workers, and intelligentsia as classes; the class which enjoys most social respect is the intelligentsia.

Most people who are not Communists prefer to use the word 'Communism' to describe the state of things, and the principles involved *in practice* in the U.S.S.R., China, and some other countries today. We object to the view that revolution of the kind which Marx described is 'inevitable' because so much of Marx's theories has been disproved by events. At the same time it is always possible, in some particular country which is economically backward, that the industrial workers may seize power in the Marxist manner. History suggests, however, that governments established by force 'for the good of the people' can only too easily turn into dictatorships of the Stalinist kind, except perhaps in cases where the people already have well-established experience of representative government.

In backward countries many admirable men and women have been inspired by the simplicity of Marxism to a faith that men can control their own social destiny, and it may well be the first time in history that such a faith has been possible in these countries. It is quite inadequate in such cases for us to object that 'Marxism' cannot cope with the variety of human motives or the complexity of history. Imperfect theories have often inspired people to desirable progress, and we may well doubt whether the U.S.S.R. could have made such great advances if her leaders, *given the circumstances of 1917,* had not been Marxists. What most of us object to is the view that nobody but Marxists can make real advances in *any* historical circumstances. The proper 'answer to Marxism' is a positive attitude, more flexible and more inclusive of non-economic factors than Marxism, which can still put first necessities first.

# 2

## THE PAST

ABOUT THE TIME when the Angles and Saxons were beginning to filter into the decaying Roman colony of Britain, people who can be recognized as Russians were colonizing the western borders of what we now know as Russia. In such districts as Novgorod, Smolensk, and Kiev, in the late fourth and fifth centuries, they paddled their canoes on the rivers, hunted the plentiful game, killed animals for food and fur, and collected wild honey. They tilled the land in the mixed forest and wooded steppe regions, very often by the primitive method of burning a patch of forest, raising a crop on the soil thus enriched with ash, and moving on in a year or so to burn another patch. There was much less good land for the early Russians than the Angles and Saxons found in Britain, and the Russian climate was a great deal more severe than the British, but there was almost no limit to the land which Russians could explore. For hundreds of years after Britain had been fully settled, peasants in many parts of Russia were still moving on from one primitive patch to another. And for this reason, along with other reasons in later history, Russians in general have been somewhat less attached to their particular patch of land than is usual elsewhere, although they have always been attached to the Russian land as a whole.

South of the forest zones, however, in the rich steppe land, life early grew more stable, and the first country which can be called Russia was established here in the ninth century. It was known as Rus, and its capital was Kiev.

The wealth of Rus was primarily in grain, and its high-way was the River Dnieper and its connections. Trade began, probably through a surplus of grain and of cattle, hides, and horses. Along the river systems from the north came a surplus of furs, timber, tar, and honey, and from the south and east came salt, wine, fruit, silk, spices, and jewels. Slaves were exchanged too, and Kiev became one of the greatest trading centres and one of the largest cities in Europe. The princes of Kiev and the neighbour-ing little states were themselves traders, and their laws laid down elaborate rules for trading and for credit. (Interest of fifty per cent. could be charged for loans of more than a year.) There was far more trade going on in Europe during the early Middle Ages than is often under-stood; the Angles and Saxons had well-developed trade, and some of their coins travelled right across Europe as far as Kiev, to be discovered there in excavations a thou-sand years later.

After the Saxons the Vikings invaded Britain, and the Vikings came to Kiev too. For Kiev controlled the water route which led, with a few short portages, from the Baltic Sea to the Black Sea and on to Byzantium, the centre of the Eastern Roman Empire. There was rich plunder for adventurers along this route, and it was some Swedish Vikings, the Varangians, who came from the Baltic to Kiev in the late ninth century. They made themselves masters of the principality and established its leadership over the surrounding districts of Rus. The dynasty they set up, the house of Rurik, became so powerful and wealthy that it was connected by marriage with many of the royal houses of Germany, Scandinavia, France, and even Britain. The city of Kiev was so rich that in 1124 it was said to have six hundred churches.

The people of Rus probably had much the same stan-dard of living as the people of Anglo-Saxon England.

Some of their farms were worked by freemen, others by slave labour, but there were no signs of the development of a feudal system, such as appeared in England well before the Norman Conquest. The princelings of Rus were often weak or at war with one another, and even when something like an overriding power was established in Kiev, the system of inheritance was made so complicated that the rule of the strong, and not of law, was often what prevailed. The Kievan Russians had assemblies—the *veche* in the towns and the *mir* in the villages—which decided many matters of local interest, and the towns were often strong enough to resist their rulers and even to expel them. However, this can hardly be counted as democracy in the modern sense, but as something more primitive. These assemblies show the deep-rooted Russian liking for community; minorities in the *veche* and the *mir* had to be persuaded to fall in with the views of the rest, or the decisions, it was felt, could not be regarded as truly communal.

At first the people of Rus worshipped Slavonic gods and the powers of nature, but Christianity reached Kiev in the ninth century, and in 988 the ruler Vladimir was baptized. He had thousands of his subjects forcibly baptized too, and he began a campaign in which pagan idols were destroyed and pagan cults were to be rooted out. Actually the peasants kept many of their old beliefs and superstitions along with their new worship, and right on into the twentieth century the Russian countryside was full of magical beliefs, witches, charms, brownies, and ancestor spirits inhabiting birch trees. In remoter places some remains of these beliefs may continue even today.

But the Russians did accept Christianity, and the Church became the chief civilizing influence in their lives. The Russian Church is one of the Orthodox or Eastern Churches, like the Greek, Serbian, Rumanian, and some others, and it prides itself on preserving the simplicity and faith of the first Christian communities. Orthodox Christians have no Pope, and they regard Roman Catholics as having obscured the true faith by elaborate organization, while Protestants, they feel, impose too much responsibility on the individual conscience. Russian Christians have always called themselves 'true believers', and have felt that their faith gave Russia a special destiny in the world ever since the Turks took Byzantium (Constantinople); the Russian Church considered itself thereafter as having taken over the leadership of true believers from the Greeks, who were now dispersed or oppressed.

The essence of the Russian Orthodox faith consists first in preserving old usages and forms, so that the original Christian spirit shall not be lost. Church buildings, for instance, should have a central dome and smaller domes at the four corners, like the earliest church in Jerusalem. But strictness of ritual has not meant strictness of law. On the contrary the Russian Church, as has frequently been said, is a Church 'of the Beatitudes rather than of the Law and the Commandments'. To make too much of the latter, it has been felt, might interfere with a proper Christian relationship between individuals. And Soviet Russians still feel that foreigners attach too much importance to laws and institutions, while foreigners, on the other hand, are maddened by the apparent inconsistency with which Soviet directives and Soviet law can be adapted to individual cases, sometimes in the direction of greater severity, sometimes of greater leniency.

After ritual, the essence of the Russian faith has always consisted in the blessed feeling of 'togetherness'. 'Where two or three are gathered together in My Name, there will I be with you'; and the Russians have rather doubted whether there could be any true Christianity without this gathering together. (An exception is made for saintly characters, who may attain holiness by a sort of Eastern asceticism, but unlike the Eastern sages they usually descend into the world's affairs again.) To the ordinary member of a Russian congregation the Western emphasis on personal striving after perfection has always been quite foreign. Confession and repentance has meant the returning of the sinner to the common fold, rather than individual salvation. Other features which have kept the Church close to the people have been that the parish priests are usually married, and that the Bible and church services are in a language which people understand.

One may perhaps wonder whether 'togetherness' would have been quite so strong in the Russian Church if the pagan Russians had not already had such a sense of community. Anyhow the blend of the two influences produced something which still seems almost ineradicable from the Russian 'national character'; it accounts for the major differences, in both the past and the present, between the Russians and ourselves. The unbelieving Englishman today still owes his attitude of personal independence in large measure to the Western Church, which fostered personal responsibility for so many centuries, while the unbelieving Russian owes his sense of brotherhood and community to the Eastern tradition.

To return, however, to the Kievan Russians. Their land was always open to invaders from the East, and they rarely showed much unity in resisting them. (Among the tribes who harassed them were the Polovtsy, who captured their Prince Igor; the story of Borodin's opera is taken from these events.) The Tartars and Mongols grew ever stronger and more ruthless, and in the thirteenth century they were brilliantly led. By 1240 Kiev was sacked and burnt, the state of Rus was destroyed, its survivors had fled north into the forests, and Russian history may almost be said to have begun all over again.

In the north cities such as Novgorod and Pskov kept their identity but, like other Russian settlements, they had to pay tribute to the all-conquering Mongols. The great leader Alexander Nevsky not only had to pay humiliating visits to the Mongol rulers; he had also to defeat attacks from the west made by Swedes, Germans, and Lithuanians. (Rus remained only an idea; part of it now belonged to Lithuania, or Lettow, where Chaucer's knight sought adventure: 'In Lettow had he reysed (raided) and in Russe.' He was a good Catholic knight and presumably wanted to campaign against the Eastern heretics.)

Moscow is not mentioned in Russian records until 1147, and for a long time it was less important than other cities in the forest, such as Vladimir. It had no local aristocracy or body of merchants, but this initial lack of importance helped in the end to make Moscow great. Princes found it easier to govern in a city where there was no opposition, and Moscow's freedom from strife brought it both trade and influential Church foundations. The Princes of Moscow gradually acquired power over other principalities, and their power was autocratic, since under the Mongol domination no other kind of power was likely to survive. Then, a century after the fall of Kiev, Ivan I of Moscow was able to persuade the Mongols that he, and he alone, was capable of collecting tribute for them from the whole of Russia. His people nicknamed him 'Moneybags', but the Mongols granted him the title of Grand Prince of Moscow. To this he himself added 'and of all Russia'. He fortified the Kremlin (the citadel of Moscow), and he established Moscow firmly as both the political and the ecclesiastical capital.

1. *A Winter Crowd in Russia.*

In 1380 the Russians felt confident enough to take on a Mongol force which far outnumbered them, and at Kulikovo in south Russia they inflicted a great defeat which meant that Russia was safe from the advance of Islam (though the Mongols remained for some time yet). This is the great battle in Russian history, parallel to the battle of Poitiers where the Moslems were thrown back from the West in 732, and the gap of 650 years between the battles is some measure of the way in which Russia had to lag behind Western Europe.

In 1480 Ivan III, or the Great, was strong enough to be able to end the Mongol domination without bloodshed, and he assumed the title of Tsar of all Russia. Ivan the Terrible (1533-84) conquered the Tartar kingdoms on his borders—Kazan, Astrakhan, and Western Siberia, but he instituted a system of government quite as savage as that of the Tartars, and at the end of his reign the country was again attacked from both south and west. In the early seventeenth century Moscow was even captured by the Poles for a while.

In spite of all, however, the Russians did have reason to feel themselves a nation, and more so probably than in Kievan times. The Church held the nation together; it was a refuge; it was the expression of the whole brotherhood of true-believing Russians; the Tsar was God's anointed representative, even though as a man he might be savage, or a nonentity, or insane, as sometimes happened.

Russia was beginning to have a few peaceful contacts with western countries; Ivan the Terrible brought in foreigners to start the first Russian printing-press and other enterprises, and in his reign English merchants formed the Muscovy Company and began to trade with

2. *Moscow Old and New*. The Red Square with the Tomb of Lenin and St. Basil's Cathedral (1560), the Kremlin wall and Spasskaya tower (1491) on right, nineteenth century commercial buildings on left, and new flats on the skyline.

B

Moscow through Archangel, along with merchants from Holland, Germany, and Denmark. (Incidentally they met with as much suspicion and difficulty as foreigners found more recently during the worst years of the Soviet period.) A few Dutchmen, Danes, and Germans also helped to improve the organization and weapons of Russian armies, and a number of Scots settled in Russia as soldiers, sailors, or doctors. Some Italian architects helped to build several of the oldest churches in the Kremlin and to develop the Moscow style of architecture. In the seventeenth century Latin began to be taught in a few schools for noblemen.

That, however, was about all so far as contact with European culture was concerned. It was, in Russian eyes, a culture of heretics, and of nations many of whom had repeatedly made war on Russia. So it did not seem to matter too much that very few Russians could read, and that for those who could there were only a few Orthodox books. (Even the ordinary Arabic numerals were not introduced until the middle of the seventeenth century.) Russia is a country which had no Renaissance, no Reformation, no free peasantry until the later nineteenth century, no independent judiciary until 1864, and only the shadow of a parliament, briefly, from 1905 to 1917, while England had already established these last three in the later Middle Ages. Russia in the seventeenth century was still in the Middle Ages in almost every respect, and in the comparatively early Middle Ages. The general standard of living was probably much the same as in the Kievan period, except for a privileged few in Moscow and a few other cities. The average standard may well have been lower than in the Kievan period, because the soil in northern Russia is less fertile than in the south; famines were frequent.

The Russians no longer had to endure the Mongol yoke. But they had serfdom and tsardom instead, and they had to endure these until 1861 and 1917 respectively. It is easy to look back with horror at these institutions and to dismiss them as 'medieval' in the sense in which we in England understand the term. But countries differ from each other much more than may appear if one studies political history only, and if two countries go through similar political stages, it does not follow that their reactions to those stages are the same, nor that those stages mean the same thing in both countries in social terms. In order to understand Russians of the past—and also, to a large extent, Russians of the present—it is particularly important to appreciate what the Russian attitude was to both serfdom and tsardom.

Tsardom was probably inevitable, since only an autocrat could have dealt with the Mongols or organized national resistance. Serfdom was probably inevitable for the same reason as in other countries—that when a military class grows up which can defend the nation as a whole against invaders, another class of the population is usually compelled in the end to till the land on its behalf. The process of compulsion took a long time in Russia, and serfdom was never either natural or acceptable to the mass of Russians. But tsardom for a long time appeared both acceptable and natural.

The reasons for the unacceptability of the one and the acceptability of the other spring from the same root—from the deeply felt egalitarianism of the Russian people. This may seem paradoxical, but an appreciation of it is essential for understanding Russians. They are egalitarian because of their ancient equality in the peasant *mir*, where decisions had to be unanimous; because of the communal traditions of their Church, trying to preserve the spirit of the first Christian brethren; and because of the good-natured, permissive way they have been brought up as children, confident in the love and tolerance of all their elders in the village, instead of being disciplined as little individuals in isolated families. They are egalitarian about *status*: to a Russian it is an insult for any man to treat another as though he were an inferior sort of human being. Even officers in Soviet labour camps, we are told by those who suffered in them, may be offended if it is suggested that in enforcing some harsh order they have not shown proper respect for prisoners as human beings. To be acknowledged as a person equal in the sight of God is the essential, and this attitude continues even though probably a majority of Russians no longer believe in God. Granted this equality of status as a human being, Russians find it easy to accept differences of rank or function; they can regard these as a matter either of practical necessity or simply of fate. One can feel this in the novels of Dostoievsky, and one can feel it in quite a brief visit to Russia today.

The tsar, however, was above all differences of rank and function, and that was one reason why he was so acceptable. During the troublous times of the late sixteenth and early seventeenth centuries, when the succession was often in doubt, and at one time there was no tsar at all, some of the noble Muscovite families tried to establish their own dynasty on the throne. But they were not going to descend to the level of the Polish nobles, who elected one of their own number each time the throne became vacant. What the Russians wanted was a supreme personification of authority raised far above them all. 'If the tsar himself acts unjustly, it is his will,' they said. 'It is easier to suffer injury from the tsar than from one's brother.'

During the troublous period from 1584 to 1613 an important part was played by the Assembly of the Land, a body resembling the States-General of France. Some of its members were elected, but it did not develop into anything like the beginning of representative government. It held the field until it had agreed on an acceptable tsar, the sixteen-year old Michael Romanov (1613-45), and afterwards lapsed into insignificance, while the Romanov dynasty remained on the imperial throne until 1917.

Tsardom came to mean the enforcement of service to the state—in the first place military service—from the landed class, and in theory from all classes. A bureaucracy grew up to ensure the carrying out of imperial decrees and many of these bureaucrats had power to act as both prosecutor and judge; there were no independent law courts to which people could appeal. The country was loaded with a hierarchy of officials whose rank and function had to be respected, but they were not thought of as superior creatures in their own right; they were merely agents of the tsar, and often agents who abused the tsar's power and whom, it was believed, the tsar would punish if he knew of their crimes. These crimes, however, were not felt to infect the reputation of the tsar himself.

The institution of serfdom did not spring from the tsars. There were many kinds of serfdom, which arose through custom, local necessity, and local enforcement. Although the authority of the tsar was firmly established by the early sixteenth century, it took more than another century to make serfdom complete. Peasants were escaping from the system the whole time—into the fertile southern lands bordering on the Tartars (where they became known as Cossacks), into the northern forests where serfdom never penetrated, or into Siberia. It was not merely intrepid individuals but families and even whole villages which migrated. Many landowners had a desperate search for labour, and serfs were for a long time allowed to change their landlord at stated times, so long as they had paid their taxes. It was not until 1649 that they lost the last remnant of a legal right to escape.

Serfs could be bought and sold, the status of serf was

hereditary, and under bad masters they might be brutally treated and their womenfolk wronged. But serf and land-owner in church continued to take communion from the same cup, and the serfs never ceased to feel that the land should belong to those who actually tilled it. The peasants kept their *mir* to regulate the tilling of their own little plots and the life of the village in general. In some part or other of Russia there were peasant revolts, or at least riots, almost every year, and these continued even after the Emancipation of 1861. In the seventeenth and eighteenth centuries the revolts led by Bolotnikov, Stenka Razin, Bulavin, and Pugachov amounted to local civil wars.

In respect of peasant independence, therefore, one needs to qualify the idea of Russia as being typically ' medieval '. Serfdom was not feudal; there was no hierarchy of lords and overlords, tenants and undertenants. Estates were mostly small; Ivan the Terrible had seen to it that none of his nobles held land in such large blocks as might form a base for power in competition with his own. And there was unlimited room for the bold to run away from their masters. In Siberia small bands, some consisting of the tsar's soldiers or convicts, and some of runaways, fought their way east against native tribes, founded the city of Irkutsk on Lake Baikal, and actually reached the shores of the Pacific as early as 1640. The Russian peasants in general were not cowed, though they were shrewd enough at giving the appearance of being cowed when necessary; neither did they develop such a chip on the shoulder as some other subject peoples have done. In our own time the Russians have often had to appear submissive, but they are still not cowed, nor have they much of a chip. The fact that their serfdom started so late is even more important than the fact that it ended only in 1861; the feeling of a freer, if primitive, kind of peasant life was preserved through the years of serfdom, right into the twentieth century.

Yet for all the persistence of antique ways of life, Russia was unable to stay completely isolated from the course of history in Western Europe. Among the few Russians who knew about the West there were some, in the seventeenth century, who wanted to break down their country's isolation, as well as many who feared the effects of foreign contamination. The modern history of Russia is largely the story of the battle between these two tendencies—which were not uncommonly found in one and the same individual. More and more Russians came to know that their country was backward, but they often feared to import the ways of foreigners who were not true believers, and who seemed to have so little understanding of the true nature of human society as demonstrated in the great, warm, family-like Russian community under its anointed tsar.

The Russian community suffered a severe shock in the sixteen-fifties, when the Church underwent the Great Schism, which might be described as a Reformation in reverse. For while in Western Europe sects were splitting off further and further ' to the left ' of the Mother Church, in Russia trouble arose because of a movement ' to the right ', back towards the Orthodox origins. The Church of Moscow had proudly assumed leadership of the Orthodox world for two centuries, and other Orthodox peoples, oppressed as they were by Turks or Poles, applied increasingly to Moscow for material help. The strict preservation of ritual was fundamental for all the Orthodox, and it now appeared that the ritual of the Greeks, who had introduced Russia to the faith, differed in some respects from the ritual observed by the Russians. Both parties maintained that their own tradition was the pure one. The differences were mostly minute—whether ' Alleluia ' was to be said twice or thrice at certain parts of the service, for instance—but the principle was a very great one. Was Moscow to remain the leader, or were the Greeks, as the earliest Christians, still to carry authority in their diminished and oppressed state?

The Patriarch Nikon, head of the Russian Church, announced to the consternation of his people that the Greeks were right, and the tsar supported him. A large group of clergy and laymen rebelled against the Patriarch—an unheard-of event in Russian Church history—and were persecuted when they would not conform. Eventually they split off to form the sect of the Old Believers and keep the old Russian forms of ritual. Through persecution the Old Believers were forced into something like the same social position as Nonconformists were in England. There are still some of them in Soviet Russia, they have a few churches of their own, and they remain austere, for example in their ban on tobacco.

The position of the Russian Church after 1667 was thus much weakened. It had lost part of its membership, and its power over the rest was now partly due to the support of the tsar. Complete surrender to the state followed; Peter the Great did not like the autonomy of the Church, and in 1721 he abolished the office of Patriarch and put the Church under the authority of a Synod nominated by himself. One member of the Synod, who wielded the effective authority, was a layman, and the Church remained in this subordinate position until the last tsar had been deposed in 1917. There were no more Church leaders to speak out against tyranny as there had sometimes been earlier, and naturally enough, nearly all the reforming movements which flourished in the nineteenth century were either opposed to the Church or wanted its drastic reform. Russia remained, however, the champion of the Orthodox. Her intervention on their behalf against the

Turks or Austrians was always feared by the rest of Europe as likely to upset the balance of power, and it was regarded as a noble duty for Russians to volunteer to fight with other Orthodox countries against the Turks, as Vronsky did at the end of *Anna Karenina*.

Peter the Great (1682-1725) was the most powerful figure in Russian history until Lenin and Stalin. He changed Russia more than Napoleon changed France. A man of great size and strength, he would wrestle with his own soldiers and execute rebels with his own hands. Before he became tsar he spent much of his time in the suburb of Moscow where foreigners lived, and when he was on the throne he preferred the company of soldiers, sea captains, craftsmen, and intelligent foreigners to court society. He travelled in Holland, France, and England— the first tsar to leave his country—collected seamen and craftsmen, mostly from Holland, and worked at crafts himself.

Peter dragged Russia out of the Middle Ages into Europe, and spared neither himself nor his people so that his country should make a mark in the world. For almost the whole of his reign he was at war against Russia's traditional enemies, the Swedes and Turks. The Swedes were led by the heroic warrior-king Charles XII, and when he was decisively defeated by Peter at Poltava in 1709 all Europe knew that Russia was a power to be reckoned with. Peter created a standing army, he created the Russian navy on Dutch models, and as a result of his conquests Russia was for the first time able to use the Baltic freely as a highway to the outside world. He turned his back on medieval Moscow and built in a few years, at great cost in human life, the stately and beautiful capital of St. Petersburg, Russia's 'window on Europe'. He made his nobles shave off their beards and forsake their old Russian gowns for the ordinary European dress of the period. He started newspapers. He started Russia's first schools apart from the Church, and he founded the Academy of Sciences. He subordinated the Church to the state on the model of the Lutheran countries which he had visited. Trade with foreign countries expanded enormously through St. Petersburg, and Moscow declined. Britain became dependent on Russia for naval stores of timber, hemp, flax, and tar. Western habits and Western learning poured into Russia in a flood.

In Russia progress has usually trickled very slowly for long periods, and then some figure of exceptional force has pushed the country in a generation through stages which elsewhere might spread over fifty or a hundred years. For this reason such leaders as Ivan the Terrible (in spite of his later crimes) and especially Peter the Great are honoured in Soviet Russia still. St. Petersburg is now called Leningrad, but anything associated with Peter is still one of the 'sights' of the city, and there is even a Soviet 'musical' about him, called *The Tobacco Captain*.

After Peter's death there was some retreat from the discipline he had imposed, but the westernization remained—though agriculture and the condition of the mass of the people had been little affected. During the eighteenth century the Russian court and aristocracy came more and more to resemble those of other European countries. All the arts began to flourish, especially under the influence of Catherine the Great (1762-96), when French influence became predominant. The upper class adopted French as their second, and sometimes even as their first language. (This tradition continued until the Revolution, and one may still meet old people in Moscow who were brought up in it.) Russian literature began, with rather formal writers on classical French models, such as Derzhavin and Fonvisin. The Russian ballet began, and alongside the ikon painters there were now Russian painters working in the styles of Western Europe. Education and the sciences were formed more on German models, and Russian education has always preserved rather German traditions of thoroughness and the amassing of facts. Catherine, who was a woman of great character and vitality, corresponded with foreign leaders of thought such as Voltaire, Diderot (who visited her), D'Alembert, and Grimm. She liked intellectual discussion, but she did not encourage criticism unless she could control it. However, the rationalism of the French *Encyclopédistes* and the revolutionary ideas of Rousseau had their result before the end of the century: small circles of the upper class became critical of their country, and showed something of a political as well as a moral conscience about the state of the masses.

The tragic effect of Peter's westernization was that it decisively separated the privileged few from the majority —separated them in culture and education and to some extent in social attitudes. The smaller gentry often remained, as most of them had been during the earlier years of serfdom, as illiterate and primitive as their own peasants. In 1762 the landowners secured from the feeble Peter III the abolition of all obligation to service; only the serfs now had obligations—to till their masters' land, to pay poll tax, and to serve in the army. In 1773-5 they broke out in the greatest of all peasant revolts, led by Pugachov, of which we read in Pushkin's *The Captain's Daughter*.

Yet although the general condition of the serfs remained miserable, they could not be quite unaffected by westernization. Some of them were forced into the army, often for twenty-five years, and if they returned safely to their village they brought at least some scraps from the outside world. Gifted serfs might be formed into rich men's orchestras or theatre companies; some of them kept accounts or practised the new crafts, and these gifted ones were sometimes given their freedom. A few masters began to learn improved methods from foreign agriculture, and some started industrial enterprises. There were even serf inventors. Most serfs had freedom to trade if they could win any surplus from their pitiful resources, and it now became possible for a few of them to amass money and even to buy their freedom.

The universal genius Lomonosov (1711-65), after whom the University of Moscow is named, was the son of a peasant from the White Sea, where serfdom did not reach. He studied in Germany, was elected to the Academy of Sciences, and by the standards of his time was as distinguished in literature as he was in the sciences.

Catherine's Russia was not simply aping the West; she was the proud Empress of a country whose troops Europe had to respect after they defeated Frederick the Great and occupied Berlin in the Seven Years' War (1756-63). Three times during Catherine's reign Russia, Prussia, and Austria seized parts of Poland, until in 1795 Polish independence disappeared altogether. The Turks and Tartars were finally driven out of the south, and all the fertile steppes down to the Black Sea were now open to settlement, largely by free men.

Under Alexander I (1801-25) the power and prestige of Russia rose higher than at any time until the recent years of Soviet government. For in the Napoleonic Wars, though Russia suffered defeat at first like every other country, and came to terms many times with the Emperor, it was the Russians who in 1812 first destroyed a huge French army. In the beginning they had to retreat before the *Grande Armée*, which with its 500,000 men was larger than the Russian regular force. But almost the whole nation rose in resistance: the peasants showed that though serfs they were still Russians. Three-quarters of Moscow went up in flames, and the wily Kutuzov harried the French as they had to retreat. Three months of winter and peasant guerrillas reduced the *Grande Armée* to pitiful bands of fugitives, and a year later the Emperor Alexander, at the head of his Guards, rode into Paris, which had been inviolate for centuries.

This war is known in Russia as the Great Fatherland War, and if one wants to have some idea of what it is to be a Russian one must try to imagine, among other things, how one would feel if England had had to endure the devastation of the French in 1812 and of the Germans in 1941-44, and how victorious, beyond all reasonable expectation, one's countrymen in the end had been. The Russian victory over Napoleon was not even due to a great preponderance of manpower, such as Stalin's Russia had over the Germans; in 1812 the population of Russia was probably only about a third larger than that of France. So the blatant music of Tchaikovsky's *1812* overture seems right and proper to Russians. One has only to read *War and Peace* in order to penetrate right into the period. Even the film of Tolstoy's novel conveys something of the feeling; it is one of the few American films which has been allowed on Soviet screens.

After their victory the peasants hoped they had earned the right to their freedom and the ownership of their land, and the progressives among the gentry looked for a liberal constitution. But though Alexander had been 'interested' in liberal ideas, especially those from England, he could not bring himself to westernize Russian institutions. His minister Speransky (another gifted man of humble origin) drew up complete schemes for representative government both nationally and locally, and for separating the administration from the judiciary, but scarcely any of his plans were carried out. Many officers had picked up political ideas from France, America, or

England, and at Alexander's death they revolted, in the 'Decembrist' rising, demanding the abolition of serfdom and a radical liberalization of government. They were easily (and savagely) suppressed, since most of the army remained loyal, but their example remained; theirs was the first organized movement against the tsarist system. The peasant revolts had never been revolts against the tsar, and Pugachov had even given himself out to be the legitimate claimant to the throne.

The suppression of the Decembrists gave the new tsar a perfect opportunity to show from the start what sort of an autocrat he was. Nicholas I (1825-55) was a martinet at the head of an Empire, and he built up the prototype of a police state. Ostensibly his repression and censorship were imposed by a paternal tsar for the good of his people, so that they should not give themselves unnecessary distress by seeking to move out of their station, and the police were supposed to be welcomed as providing a direct channel from the people to the tsar, past the bureaucracy!

In foreign affairs Nicholas became known as 'the gendarme of Europe'. He did his implacable best, in alliance with Prussia and Austria, to repress liberal or constitutional movements in Eastern or Central Europe. His policy continually threatened Turkey, and was a menace to the Middle East and the overland route to India. Western Europe in general, and particularly Britain, looked on Russia throughout the century as a reactionary, police-ridden tyranny and an enemy in every way to freedom, ruling by the whips of the Cossacks and the threat of deportation to Siberia. When the Crimean War broke out in 1853 its immediate causes were of little significance; it was a war against Russia as a menace to the East and against Russian tyranny, much more than a war to support Turkey.

The English, French, and Turks were so inept in this

war that they hardly deserved to win, but the police state of Nicholas proved even more incapable. Nicholas died, amid the widespread rejoicing of his subjects, just before the end of the war, and as he died he knew that both his home and his foreign policies had failed. Russia, however, gained from defeat, for the next tsar had to carry out reforms. This was the first of three major defeats which helped to bring the old system to an end—the Crimean defeat which led to the abolition of serfdom, the defeat in the Russo-Japanese War which led to the granting of a constitution, and defeat in the First World War which brought about the two Revolutions of 1917.

From the time of Catherine onwards, in fact, there was a growing head of revolutionary steam pent up in Russia. It increased mightily during the reign of Nicholas, although the censorship prohibited the printing of anything remotely suggesting reform. Pushkin, who suffered all his life under police surveillance or exile, once offered to edit for Nicholas a periodical which would bring men of talent 'closer to the government', but his offer was refused—no doubt because Pushkin was already known not only as a writer of genius but as a man of 'dangerously' liberal views, and in a few of his works the prophet of a freer Russia. The great age of Russian literature, which had begun under Alexander, continued more brilliantly under Nicholas, though some works had to wait for publication until the next reign. Pushkin and Lermontov wrote some of their greatest works; Gogol wrote his satirical play *The Inspector-General* and his comic masterpiece about the serf-owners, *Dead Souls*; Tolstoy, Turgenev, Goncharov, Nekrassov, and Dostoievsky all published their first work in this period. From now onwards the world respected not only Russian power but Russian literature and music, and foreigners felt the more sympathy for those suffering under tsarism.

The young Dostoievsky was unwise enough to join a private circle for the discussion of political questions, and in 1849 was arrested and, with other members of the circle, taken out for public execution. They were reprieved at the very last second; the experience had been meant only to teach them 'a severe lesson'. One of them went mad, and the others were marched off for long sentences in Siberian camps.

In such an atmosphere nearly all men of intelligence and education—except for the bureaucracy—were against the existing system. The word *intelligentsia* developed a special meaning in nineteenth century Russia; it did not merely imply intellectuals, but intellectuals who took up the proud task of reform. Belinsky (1810-48), the first great Russian critic, made literary criticism into a public force, and is honoured in Soviet Russia largely because he argued that art should serve society, and that the greatness of Russian literature in his own age was that it undertook to do so. Herzen (1812-70), one of the greatest Russian writers, had to spend most of his life in exile because of his revolutionary activities. Although a serf-owner, he was the father of idealistic, utopian Russian socialism, and he is highly honoured for this in Russia today. Bakunin (1814-76) was an aristocrat who was involved in the early socialist movements but was eventually expelled because he preached in fact a destructive anarchism: when all existing social and political forms had been destroyed, the natural goodness of man, it was alleged, would form a free and noble society. This attitude became known as nihilism, and some of its followers took to assassination and bomb-throwing as means of hastening on the millennium.

Belinsky, Bakunin, and in his early days Herzen were 'westernizers', and there was a strong movement against them by the 'Slavophils', who held that Russia, far from needing to learn from the West, had spiritual resources of her own which the West could not hope to rival. The Orthodox faith and the unique native institution of the *mir* would produce a superior civilization if only the bureaucratic government machine could be removed. The Slavophils had an idealistic faith in the Russian peasant, and looked back to the days of a purer Russian culture before Peter the Great. Eventually many of them became organized in a kind of agricultural socialist party —the Social Revolutionary Party—which had much support among the peasants. Its old Russian mistrust of 'laws and institutions', however, and its childlike attachment to terrorism made it a very unsuitable party for the twentieth century.

There was a ferment of reforming ideas, programmes, manifestoes, and tracts during the last century of tsarism, and one can read in Dostoievsky's *The Devils* (or *The Possessed*) how fantastic some of these could be. (Dostoievsky himself was a Slavophil.) Some good thinking went into the best of this reforming work, and if Russia had had anything like Western governmental institutions at this period there might not eventually have been a Revolution. The ideological ferment remained a ferment because so little opportunity of practical reforming activity was open to educated Russians. To get 'bread, or a pair of boots' was the problem for the mass of Russians, and because a practical solution seemed impossible, many educated people only gossipped superficially about ideas of reform. In Tchehov's plays the apparently idle characters, talking in sententious clichés, are satirically meant to point the predicament in which intelligent men found themselves.

Under Alexander II (1855-81) the press indeed had some freedom, and from 1855 right up to 1917 there was more liberty for the press than at any time either before or since; it was possible to print political opinions if one was prepared to run the risk—a very real one—of fines and confiscation.

The great reforms of Alexander were the emancipation of the serfs in 1861, the establishment of an independent judicial system for the first time in 1864, the establishment of elected local councils (*zemstva*), and some development of primary and secondary education. The new judicial arrangements were excellent, but Alexander III (1881-94) clamped down again in the old way and put ' political ' cases or cases ' which might excite the public ' back into the power of the police. The *zemstva* did some good work in education, public health, and agriculture, but they were too much dominated by the gentry, and in 1890 the peasants' share in their election disappeared.

The emancipation of the serfs, however, once done could not be undone. It was a gigantic operation, and it was not at all unexpected. Ever since Catherine's time serfdom had been regularly acknowledged—and not only by reformers—as the great Russian evil; the difficulty was to organize a settlement which would affect forty million people. It took twenty years from 1861 to carry out the change. The peasants had to pay redemption annuities to the landlords for the land which they received, and the landlords still retained much for themselves. The peasant land was not as a rule assigned to individuals, and the peasants would have been surprised if it had been; it was assigned to peasant households organized in communes—about 120,000 of them over all Russia. The commune was now made responsible to the state for taxes, and it continued, as for centuries past, to decide the working of the land, the assignment and reassignment of family strips, and other local matters, by a sort of ' taking the feeling of the meeting '. The *mir* was not an elected body, but it provided the only experience of self-government which most Russians ever had. After the emancipation the yield of peasant farming did not much improve, there were severe famines in several years, and the redemption payments had to be scaled down and eventually cancelled.

So the peasants had their freedom from serfdom but not freedom from debt. Most of them thought they had been cheated, and there were riots, murders of landowners, and burnings of their houses every year. The landowners mostly did not adjust themselves to the change in society, but sold their land bit by bit in order to live, like Madame Ranevsky in *The Cherry Orchard*. The intelligentsia remained dissatisfied with the inadequacy of even Alexander II's reforms, largely because there was still no representative central government. (Even the landowners were not consulted in any representative way when the emancipation took place.) The intelligentsia were also indignant at the restrictions still imposed on the universities, where reforming ideas were bred. In 1881 Alexander was assassinated by a member of a Slavophil terrorist organization. It is impossible to find any justification for this crime; one can only regard Alexander II as a victim to the age-old Russian tragedy of ' too little and too late '. The assassination naturally set back the clock once more; Alexander III reimposed much of the old tyranny. Then in 1894 there succeeded the last tsar of all, Nicholas II, a stupid and feeble man who had just enough character, particularly when egged on by his German wife, to be obstinate when he should have had the sense to give way to reform.

At the emancipation in 1861 about five-sixths of Russians were peasants, and by 1917 the proportion was still almost as great—probably four-fifths. The minority still consisted partly of bureaucrats, landowners, soldiers, merchants, craftsmen, fishermen, servants, priests and monks, but the great difference in 1917 was that it included a much increased number of workers in industry—at least five million.

Industry developed late in Russia like everything else, but in the last twenty years before the Revolution it was growing very fast indeed; there were more enterprises in Russia employing over 1,000 men than there were in America at that time. There had been a certain amount of industry in Russia for several centuries, but it did not fit at all well into the restricted patterns of the tsarist state. There were state monopolies, of alcohol and salt for example, as early as the seventeenth century. Peter the Great established mining settlements, particularly in the rich mineral districts of the Urals, and in the eighteenth century Russia was for a time the greatest producer of iron ore in Europe. But the labour force consisted mostly of serfs or prisoners, and even when private companies were formed, the capital came mostly from the state; in Peter's time it often came with a compulsory service order to the gentry, who were put in charge! Textile factories for cotton and flax grew up from the early nineteenth century onwards, with British and German help, and one of the few useful acts of Nicholas I was to make things easier for them. Some factories were run by the large landowners with the labour of their own serfs. But landowners, though they might be rich, could not escape from the land, and it was impossible for industry to develop properly until the serfs were free to work where they liked, and landowners were free to do what they liked with their capital. Some factories were already run by the hired labour of free workers, and they were much more successful than those worked by serfs. Some landowners were able to prove the superiority of hired agricultural labour on their own estates, and all this had a big influence in hastening on the emancipation.

The first effect of the emancipation on industry, however, was that many factories had to close down. Industrial life was so miserable that both serfs and hired men went back to the land which they believed was now theirs. But conditions at home, they found, were no better than what they had left behind, and in winter often worse, so that in sheer desperation men drifted back to the towns again. Labour was thus freely available for the first time for Russian industry, and foreign capital—French, Belgian, and English—came flowing in too. In a short time there was an industrial proletariat of two million or so which was suffering all the evils of the early English Industrial Revolution and worse—long hours, pittance wages often paid in kind, child labour, and accommodation very often in barracks provided by the employer, with no hope of any other home for men, women, or children. Later there was some regulation by Factory Acts, but inspection was weak, and conditions on the whole were not much better by 1917, although industry had developed so fast that the national income doubled between 1900 and that year. One can read of this industrial squalor and misery in the novels of Gorky, and Soviet Russians know of it from the experience of their own elders. And because under Communism Soviet Russians have had their material conditions lately—though only lately—much improved, they are apt to believe that workers in non-Communist countries must still have to endure the same sort of misery which their own fathers had to suffer.

During the later nineteenth century not only human brutality but outworn laws and customs pressed unbearably hard, so that there was very great unrest in both town and country, and even more violence than usual. Peasants who migrated to the towns were often still regarded as members of their village commune, and out of their pitiful industrial wages they were legally bound to contribute their share of the village taxes. Arrears of tax grew, like arrears of the redemption payments, until they had to be abolished to stave off revolution. Revolution did almost take place, in fact, in 1905, when Russia lost the disastrous Russo-Japanese War. This war had been undertaken partly because of Russia's ambitions in Manchuria and her determination to keep other powers away from China, and partly because it was thought that unrest at home would be stilled. But Russia was in no state to fight such a war, and the attempt to divert the attention of the masses recoiled upon the head of the tsar.

Nearly three million workers came out on strike in 1905, and there were mutinies in the army and navy. (Two of these have since become celebrated in the films *Battleship Potemkin* and *We of Kronstadt*.) Some strikes were against bad conditions and some were political strikes against brutal government repression. The workers realized their strength and, encouraged by the Social-Democratic Party, set up councils elected by themselves which were called by the ordinary Russian word for ' council '—*soviet*. This was the first appearance of Soviets in the contemporary sense, and it is one of the reasons why Soviet historians sometimes refer to the disturbances of 1905 as ' the First Revolution '. The tsar had refused a constituent assembly, said the manifesto of the Soviets, and there was no alternative but to strike. Nicholas indeed had to do something, and quickly. He issued a Manifesto promising the fundamental liberties, votes for all, and an election for a national assembly. But though some liberals hailed the Manifesto as a great milestone in Russian history, the workers on the whole distrusted its vagueness; they went on strike again, and the events of the next few years proved them right. In 1905, however, they could achieve nothing against military force, the strikes fizzled out, and the Soviets were suppressed—in Moscow only after many days of fighting, which provided some practice in civil war. The Soviets were not forgotten; in the fifty days of their existence they had set up a nation-wide organization. The government now realized the strength of the workers, and retaliated by making their political activities almost impossible during the next decade, and by keeping troops always on hand in case of trouble.

There was some halting political progress, in three major fields, during the last years of Nicholas II. Some-thing of a consultative assembly—the Duma—was set up in 1906, though it was made clear that the divine right and absolute veto of the tsar were not affected, and that government would be carried out, as before, by his minis-ters, who were not responsible to the Duma. The Duma had some financial powers, however, and it provided, for practically the first time in Russia, a debating chamber and a channel for grievances. Voting for the Duma was arranged so that it should be dominated by conservative forces, but the First Duma so frightened the tsar and his prime minister, Stolypin, that they dissolved it; they were frightened by the Second Duma too, which included many Socialist members, and they revised the laws so that the Third Duma and the Fourth (and last) were over-whelmingly upper-class and conservative.

Education was already spreading fast, particularly through the work of the *zemstva*. A national programme of elementary schooling was put in hand in 1908, and by 1914 half the children between six and eleven years of age were attending school. The universities, however, were still subject to repression and suspicion.

In 1906 Stolypin produced a law which enabled the peasants to opt out of their communes and build up individual farms, or alternatively to leave for the city as completely free men. The aim was to encourage the ' strong and enterprising ', and it did encourage the beginnings of what might have become a class of tough individual farmers. But tradition was very strong, there were too many peasants for the land as it was, and in 1917 five-sixths of the land was still held communally on the old strip system. In Western Europe one of the most deep-seated traditions, and one still partly responsible for the independent spirit of townspeople as well as countrymen, is the tradition of independent farming by men who own their land and are responsible to no one else. It is this, for instance, which makes the Englishman's home his castle. In Russia, however, this development never got very far; the old feeling of communal responsibility was carried through the Revolution and helped to form Soviet society.

Russia was now one of the world's great trading countries, and her commercial prosperity continued to grow at a rapid rate; for a time she was the world's largest oil producer. Millions were made out of wheat, beet sugar, and the metal industries, and some of the millionaires collected Impressionist paintings or supported the work of Stanislavsky and Diaghilev in the theatre and ballet. Progressive-minded merchants and some of the gentry founded a liberal party, the 'Cadet' Party, which had some weight in the Duma. The Social Revolutionaries had support among the peasants and some intellectual circles, but still clung to the ideas of the peasant commune; the Social Democrats were strong among the industrial workers, but worked under great restrictions.

The political and economic progress in these years might have had important and permanent results if it had not been for World War I. In 1914 Russia became involved because of her ancient rivalry with Austria in the Balkans, and because of her alliance with France and Britain, but not all the tsar's advisers were in favour of the war. The country was ill-prepared, and the Germans inflicted staggering defeats, though there were some Russian successes against the Austrians. Russian industry, for all its rapid growth, could not provide the quantities of guns, ammunition, rifles, or even maps or boots which the army needed, and there was not enough transport to deliver such supplies to the front if they had been forthcoming. Those in charge of the war effort—and they changed very often— were almost all incompetent. The Duma protested so vigorously that the Tsar prorogued it and, incredible as it may seem, for over a year most of the major decisions about the war were taken by the tsarina and her favourite, the dissolute priest Rasputin. Late in 1916 Rasputin was assassinated by some patriotic noblemen, and the Duma met again. Prices had risen catastrophically, supplies of food and necessities were breaking down, and there were hundreds of strikes both economic and political in intent. Soldiers and sailors began to mutiny or desert, and by March 1917 not a single army unit could be found which would fire upon fellow-Russians. The tsar's most loyal advisers told him that revolution was unavoidable, but he still refused demands for reform of government, until his own soldiers joined the crowds demonstrating in the streets, and he was forced to abdicate.

The March Revolution—which Soviet historians call the Bourgeois Revolution—was a universal movement of the nation against the tsar and the tsarist régime. No one but his own household—and not even all of them—supported the tsar. The Governments of Britain, France, and the United States recognized the Provisional Russian Government which was formed, and their press hailed the Revolution as a triumph for the forces of liberty.

To overthrow was easy; to build afresh was another matter, and the war continued disastrously. The Provisional Government consisted of conservatives and bourgeois, except for Kerensky, who was a Social Revolutionary. They arrested the tsar, proclaimed a republic, and promised universal suffrage and land for the peasants, but this had to wait until a popularly elected Constituent Assembly could meet. The industrial workers' organizations distrusted the Provisional Government, and they set up a Soviet of workers and soldiers in the capital to criticize and eventually to challenge it.

The Soviet was composed of representatives of the Social Revolutionaries and of the two wings of the Social Democrats—the Bolsheviks and the Mensheviks—to explain which it is necessary to go back to the turn of the century. The Russian Social-Democratic Party had been founded in 1898. It was different from the other, usually vague and over-idealistic, progressive organizations. Its principles were those of Marx; it believed that revolution by the industrial working class was the only way to socialism, that such a revolution could only take place after a bourgeois revolution had overthrown the autocracy, and that strict party organization and discipline were needed, not the sporadic acts of terrorism which the Social Revolutionaries still favoured. The Party was small and had to work illegally. In 1903 its Congress had to meet in London, and it was here that Lenin made his great powers of leadership and organization felt; he obtained a majority for his programme of a small party, under iron discipline, which should lead the workers and take advantage of every turn of events to forward its aims. Lenin's faction were henceforth known as Bolsheviks—a name derived from the word for 'majority', while the Mensheviks took their name from the word for 'minority'. The Mensheviks favoured more freedom for members in their interpretations of Marxism, while Lenin insisted on unwavering obedience to policy dictated by the leadership. Although the Mensheviks were in a minority at this Congress, they had at that time more support among the Russian workers than the Bolsheviks had.

Lenin was in exile for many years before 1917, but after the March Revolution the German Government helped him to return to Russia, in the hope that he would still further weaken the resistance of the Russian armies. In June, when he addressed the National Congress of Soviets, many laughed when he declared that the Bolshevik Party was the only party ready to take on the responsibility of government, on the basis of immediate peace, exposure of the imperialistic plans of the Allies, and ' All Power to the Soviets '. In July an armed rising supported by the Bolsheviks failed, and Lenin had to go into hiding. Almost every week there were fresh shifts among groups trying for power in the capital, while in the country the peasants were seizing the land for themselves. The Bolsheviks attracted more and more support because their programme seemed concrete and immediate, and in September they gained a majority in the St. Petersburg (or Petrograd) Soviet.

On November 7th (October 25th by the old calendar which was then still used in Russia) the Bolsheviks overthrew the Provisional Government after very little fighting, and they secured power for good in this second, Bolshevik, Revolution of 1917. The Soviet nominated a Government of People's Commissars, with Lenin at the head and Trotsky in charge of foreign affairs.

At first the world failed to understand that the October Revolution was more than just another rearrangement of parties, and the Bolsheviks themselves were not altogether sure that this was not another rehearsal, as in 1905. However, on their second day of power they decreed that ' all private ownership of land is abolished forever '; all mineral resources, forests, and water of national importance were transferred to the State; and on the same day they appealed to all the belligerent nations to declare an armistice. They met with no response, and to the alarm of the Allies began to negotiate a separate peace with Germany. In March the Germans permitted them to sign the ruinous treaty of Brest-Litovsk, by which Russia had to surrender forty-four per cent. of her population and a quarter of her territory. It was typical of Lenin that he was able to drive through the acceptance of this treaty against heavy opposition within his own party. Peace was the first and basic condition before anything else could be undertaken, and in its ruthless disregard of sacrifice and its putting of first things first the signing of the treaty was a forecast of the major actions of the Soviet Government for forty years to come. (Actually a good deal of the lost territory returned to Russia when Germany collapsed in November 1918, but the Baltic Republics and a large western region did not, and one of the first Soviet aims when the Second World War began was to see that these areas were recaptured or reabsorbed.)

Meanwhile the Bolsheviks decided, against the opinion of some of their party, to hold elections for the National Assembly which had been promised by the Provisional Government. It was felt that the Bolsheviks were not yet strong enough to dispense with an election, but every effort was made to see that they should get a majority. Some of these efforts were far from legitimate, but this election may still be called the only free election by universal suffrage which was ever held in Russia. The result was that the Social Revolutionaries won more than half the seats, while the Bolsheviks got only a quarter. The Soviet therefore dissolved the Assembly after it had met for only one day. All political parties but the Bolsheviks were now outlawed, except some left wing groups who were allowed a certain freedom until 1922.

Government was now not only by the 'dictatorship of

the proletariat', but by the dictatorship of a minority party, and that party, by its own rules and traditions, was run by a small body of leaders. The ruling party adopted the name of 'Communist', which had been increasingly used, following on Marx; the term 'Social Democrat' disappeared, and ever since, Communists have regarded Social Democratic and Labour Parties as 'betrayers of the working class'. (As early as 1903 the Bolsheviks had said they would not hesitate 'temporarily' to abandon democratic principles in order to defend the Revolution when it arrived.)

In 1918 the Russian Communists expected the workers of other countries to join them in an international revolution, and there were some short-lived Communist successes in Hungary and Germany. It soon became clear, however, that Russia could hope for very little help in this way, and the internal situation in Russia was now very bad indeed. Decrees and dictatorship could not extract food supplies from the peasants, the conservative forces gathered heart again, and before long the country was in civil war. Siberia, the Ukraine, and Transcaucasia split off, and there was armed intervention by Britain, France, America, and Japan against the Bolsheviks. The new régime was saved largely by the genius and energy of Trotsky, who in a few months built up a new army, the Red Army, composed almost entirely of workers and poorer peasants, and inspired it to victory. Internal enemies were dealt with by the summary methods of the Commission for Combating Counter-revolution—the Cheka—which had absolute powers of arrest, life and death. By 1921 the 'Whites' were all defeated, the country was under one government again, and the Civil War was at an end. The Allies had been forced to realize that the Russians would not fight Germany any more, and that the ruthless methods and programme of the Bolsheviks did not mean that they had only small support. One may quote one of the few foreign observers on the spot, Sir Paul Dukes, who was a British secret agent and no friend to the Bolsheviks, but who has written that when the people were forced to choose between the Reds and the Whites they were in no doubt that it was the Whites they wanted least. Allied intervention had not been very great nor very effective, but the Bolsheviks naturally saw it in Marxist terms of the class war—foreign bourgeois against Russian workers.

After the Civil War industrial output was down to one-sixth of the 1914 rate, and agriculture was all but ruined. There was famine in which millions died, and for two years it was only American relief and the Red Cross which kept much of southern Russia alive.

Lenin now took another drastic step and introduced the New Economic Policy (usually known as N.E.P.), which encouraged the peasants and small capitalists to 'enrich themselves'—these very words were used—by working for their own profit and selling to the public at market prices. (The nationalization of the land and major industries remained.) In a few years the country returned to conditions so much improved that they might be called mild prosperity, and the Bolsheviks were very uneasy as to how far the retreat from socialism might go. Lenin had intended N.E.P. to be only a temporary expedient, but he died in 1924, as a result of having been shot by a woman Social Revolutionary some years earlier. The great division in the Party was now between Stalin, with his policy of 'Socialism in one country' and severe bureaucratic control, and Trotsky, who wanted the fomenting of revolution abroad so that other countries, when they turned Communist, might help Russia. Stalin's policy, brutal though it was in application, seemed to promise more progress at home. Trotsky was expelled from the Party and deported in 1929, to be murdered many years later in Mexico, probably at the orders of Stalin.

In 1928 the real socialization of Russia began, the conversion of decrees into practical results, through the beginning of the First Five Year Plan, whose scope and daring astonished the world. N.E.P. was brought to an end, and the only idea that most Russians have today of a 'bourgeois economy' is still that of the shallow, fat profiteers of the N.E.P.

Under the dictatorship of Stalin, and with the Five Year Plans ruling the economy, the country entered on a period which is so intimately bound up with the present state of things that it will be more convenient to drop the historical story here. This outline of Russian history has been intended to bring out the chief pre-Soviet influences which have played a part in forming Russian life and Russian attitudes today. Much more might usefully be said, and in particular much more about the period of the Revolution, since it is very rarely in history that so many fundamental and apparently permanent changes are started up in such a short space of time. If one reads the early speeches of the leaders and the reports of Communist Party meetings, it is clear that many of the best-known features of the Soviet régime grew up *ad hoc*, and not as a result of long-term planning from the beginning. Russia had been despised by Marx, and Russia was the last country which he would have chosen for the first proletarian revolution. Many of the early economic or political measures were simply experimental, and the full, severe growth of the dictatorship was not something which was expected from the beginning.

The Bolsheviks succeeded because they concentrated on the industrial workers instead of the backward and scattered peasants; because they had brilliant and ruthless leaders; because they recognized the importance of science; because they were prepared to make temporary enemies or temporary allies anywhere if they could gain by it; and because the other anti-tsarist parties trusted in dire emergency to the goodness of human nature, more or less, instead of taking painful practical steps.

Revolution of some kind was inevitable once Russia had entered the First World War. Without the war, the old régime might have tottered on to eventual improvement *if* the tsar had been a perceptive and adaptable man; *if* the landowners had devoted themselves to improving agriculture; *if* the peasants had had time to break out of their communes; *if* the employers had had time to discover that it paid them better to treat their workers better; *if* education had been given more time; or *if* representative institutions could have had more time to develop. If only three or four of these *ifs* could have been realized, Russia might have grown into something like the condition, perhaps, of France in the eighteen-thirties, though how well she would have lasted in a world where other countries were in the nineteen-thirties it is impossible to say.

None of this happened, and the Bolsheviks took over a country with a load of backwardness, a lost war, and a people eighty per cent. peasant—with a great fund of potential talent, no experience of practical government, rather too much experience of theory and principle, a long experience of dictatorship and brutal necessity, but fortunately very good traditions of communal co-opera-

---

3. *Some Soviet Racial Types.*
    (*a*) Siberian power station engineer.
    (*b*) Kazakh interpreter
    (*c*) Caucasian shepherd.
    (*d*) Uzbek woman and children.
4. (*a*) *View from the Lenin Hills* in front of Moscow University, over the giant Lenin Stadium.
    (*b*) *The River Dnieper near Kiev*—horizons are usually far in Russia.

СМОЛЯНИН

ДАЛЬНЕВОСТОЧНАЯ ЖЕЛЕЗНАЯ

tion and decent relations between human beings. They were all accustomed to hard work and phenomenal endurance, and the Bolsheviks demanded every shred of energy which they could produce.

5. *In the Far Eastern Province, by the Pacific, scenes are much the same as in European Russia.*
   (*a*) Old and new dwellings in Khabarovsk.
   (*b*) A wayside station on the Far Eastern Railway is just like wayside stations near Moscow.
6. (*a*) *Factory girls leaving work.*
   (*b*) *Cabbage is one of the Basic Foods.*

# 3

## FOUNDATIONS AND LIMITS

THE SOVIET UNION is the largest country in the world. It occupies about one-sixth of the land surface of the earth, and it has about one-thirteenth of the world's population. Within its borders there is more timber and probably more minerals than in any other country. It claims to have the greatest coal reserves in the world; it has oil for all its needs; it has iron, copper, and other metals and minerals for all likely purposes, though not all of them are in easily accessible places. The country can feed itself with basic foods, and in the hot southern regions it even grows enough cotton for present needs, besides most of its tea (which is the national drink), and some wine and citrus fruits. Only tropical products are wanting—rubber (which is mostly replaced by artificial rubber of good quality), and such things as coffee and cocoa which are not much consumed in Russia.

The Soviet Union is thus as good as self-supporting, and this fact, along with the great size and compactness of the country, conveys an overwhelming impression of power.

The impression given by the map, however, can be misleading. In the first place, the commonest type of world map distorts the northern part of the U.S.S.R. to a greatly exaggerated size. In the second place, although about three-quarters of the Soviet Union lies in Asia (i.e., east of the Urals and the Caspian), it is essential to realize that no more than a quarter of the population lives in this vast area, and most of them are concentrated in the industrial regions nearest the Urals. The greatest spaces on the

Soviet map are simply occupied by forest, and further north by Arctic swamps and tundra where the soil never thaws to a depth of more than a few inches. More than 40 per cent. of the country is coniferous forest, while 17 per cent. is occupied by these Arctic areas, snow-covered for nine or ten months and mosquito-ridden for the rest of the year. Another 10 per cent., mainly in the Asiatic Republics, is desert or semi-desert. And it is not only climate which is inhospitable. The great fir forests flourish on soil which is of little use for other purposes. The arable land (as can be seen from the map in the inside cover) is limited to 10 per cent of the whole area of the U.S.S.R., as against nearly 25 per cent. in the United States for example. The grazing land makes only another 10 per cent. And most of this land lies so deep within the Eurasian land mass that it gets less than 20 inches of rain a year, which is the limit usually found reliable for steady agriculture. The baking steppes of the black-earth region are rich, but drought is the great enemy, and in many parts the winter's snow must be organized for irrigation. It is only possible to extend the agricultural area by opening up districts, as in Kazakhstan and Western Siberia, which are still more susceptible to drought and often to frost as well. Altogether the Soviet Union has an average of 2·2 acres of cultivated land per head of the population, against 2·7 acres (usually of better land) in the United States.

In Britain we have enjoyed industrial prosperity for so long that it is easy to forget that the basis of any standard of living lies in agriculture. One cannot eat machines or machine products, and if, as in Britain, a country's own agriculture does not suffice, then the basis must lie in the agriculture of other countries, who are willing to exchange their surplus food for manufactured goods. But the U.S.S.R. is self-sufficient, and the Soviet Government has always intended it to be so, apart from imports of a few exceptional things already mentioned, and imports of advanced machinery to speed up the country's development. Partly because of this, and partly because of the limited arable area, the Soviet Union has had to cope with a severe form of the problem which faces every country when it industrializes—how to feed the population when a large proportion of the land workers must transfer to industry. The U.S.S.R. has made some progress with mechanization, but the productivity of its agriculture remains obstinately low—not much higher than it was under the tsars. There is enough for Soviet people to eat, but their diet is on the whole monotonous.

In industry, on the other hand, the progress of the Soviet Union since 1928 is probably greater than that which any other country has achieved in a similar period of time. According to the official estimate, industrial production increased sixteen times between 1928 and 1953. Mr. F. Seton, Lecturer in Economics at Oxford, estimates the increase as at least ten times, and suggests that capital equipment per head may have quadrupled during the period. The industrial labour force certainly quadrupled during this time—a huge operation even if the results had been less striking than they are.

There is no doubt that all this progress has been achieved by the policy of complete national planning. The Soviet Government was the first government to undertake planning of this kind, and the rest of the world has remained torn between admiration for the results and horror at some of the methods used to get them—the forced collectivization, labour camps, loss of life and liberty, and the totalitarian control. The totalitarian control bears less severely today, but there is no likelihood of its disappearing. It is not, however, the only factor which has made Soviet planning what it is. The peasant nature of the country, the lack of skilled workers of all kinds, and the whole historical and geographical inheritance have helped to make Soviet planning an individual case. If one is trying to get an answer to general questions about planning—whether it need be so rigid as in the U.S.S.R. or accompanied by such political dictatorship, or whether it can be combined to some extent with private enterprise—one will need to study for the next thirty years or so not only the U.S.S.R. but the very large number of other countries, some backward and some advanced, which also have a central planning authority—India, France, Yugoslavia, Egypt, and others.

The Bolsheviks nationalized[1] Russia's land, mines, and natural resources, banks, shops and distribution system, transport and communications because they were Marxists, and Marx taught that enterprise for private profit could only lead to increasing misery for the masses and increasing wealth for the few. But Marx had little to say about running the economy when the proletariat had seized power, and nothing to say about the problems of a

[1] The property which is nationalized in the U.S.S.R. is property in the means of production. Private property for personal use remains private property as in any other country and can be bequeathed. What is forbidden is to make money by buying goods and selling them again, or to employ others in order to make money out of their labour (though one may hire domestic servants at controlled rates.) It is legal to sell one's own property secondhand, or to sell the product of one's single-handed labour, e.g., as a craftsman or repair man. (Materials, however, may be hard to get hold of without illegally tapping government stocks.) One may make money by giving private lessons, by letting part of one's house (at a controlled rent), or by private practice as a doctor or lawyer, though one will find few takers in the latter case. In Soviet cities one can see little hand-written advertisements offering these services or sales, though they do not appear in the press. What the press often reports are sentences on ' speculators ' who have been making a profit out of buying and selling. Peasants have a much wider legal outlet for selling their own produce, which will be described a few pages further on, but any Soviet citizen, whether peasant or townsman, who appears to have acquired large sums of money is likely to find his private life investigated by the police, particularly if he seems able to live without working.

nationalized economy when four-fifths of the nation were peasants.

After the interlude of the N.E.P. period the fundamental problem for the Soviet Government was this: how to put most of the national effort into basic industries and capital goods without any rise, for years to come, in living standards for the consumer. There was some hope that the industrial workers might understand the need for austerity; it was they who had made the Revolution, and they already had evidence of what they could achieve by themselves. They could be inspired by the two great goals which the Soviet Government has always set —'to catch up with and surpass the capitalist countries', and 'to raise the material and cultural standards of the people.' Many of them could understand how consumer goods must wait upon the growth of basic industry, and most of them probably expected the Communist millennium to arrive within a comparatively short time. The peasants, however, were almost all of a different frame of mind, for in spite of the technical nationalization of the land they continued after the Revolution to sell their produce as independent farmers. In Moscow many leading Communists pointed out that the peasants would stop bringing their food to market if they were unable to buy more than a very few manufactured goods in exchange. But a more severe faction argued that the country could not survive against capitalist enemies unless priority was given, whatever it might cost, to capital goods and the military strength which could be built up with their help. The peasants must be compelled to yield up their grain for the industrial workers, and they must be compelled to yield up even more, so that it could be exported in exchange for the foreign machinery which it was essential to buy at this stage. Foreign loans, whether in cash or in kind, were of course unthinkable, since they would admit capitalist influence into the Soviet economy; (it was also very unlikely that many foreign capitalists would risk their money in the U.S.S.R. just then).

The severe faction won the day, and the peasants were forced into collectivization. At first the process was intended to be gradual, but with the help of 25,000 Communists, mostly raw and young, it was soon speeded up. Peasants who resisted, or who appeared to be 'exploiting' their neighbours by owning so much as a horse or cow, were sent to prison camps or shot. In desperation the peasants often retaliated by killing their animals, and at the end of the campaign the Government was left with half as many cattle and horses as before the Revolution, and a sullen, discontented peasantry who have mostly remained uncooperative to this day. It is now officially admitted that the methods of collectivization were unnecessarily severe; one may read something of the brutalities and stupidities of the period in the novels of the doyen of Soviet authors, Sholokhov.

A collective farm is a village or group of neighbouring villages with land which averages, over the whole country, about 15,000 acres in extent. The land is owned by the Government but leased to the collective farm (*kolkhoz*) in perpetuity, and a map of the area, and the title to the land, remain in the possession of the farm committee. Every family has a small plot for its own use, but more than nine-tenths of the land is cultivated communally with the help of machines which nowadays belong to the collective. The members of each collective are supposed to elect a chairman or manager, but in practice he is often appointed from above and may have no great qualifications in agriculture. His political 'drive' may thus be cancelled out by his ignorance, which makes it easier for the peasants to bamboozle him. The first duty of the collective—often referred to as a 'sacred duty'—is to deliver the quotas of grain, potatoes, cabbages, flax, cotton, etc., demanded by the plan for the district. For years the peasants were paid miserable rates for these deliveries, but under the present régime they receive much more; the total cash income of the *kolkhozy* was more than doubled in the first four years after Stalin's death. The collective farmers (*kolkhozniky*) are paid shares of the income, partly in cash and partly in kind, according to the number of workdays they put in, but they also devote a good deal of time to their own plots.

The individual plots rarely amount to more than an acre per family and are usually much smaller, but they are a very important item in Soviet economy and society. They were granted to the peasants as a concession in the later days of collectivization, and complaints that the peasants spend too much time on them have never ceased. On these plots they raise vegetables, fruit, eggs, rabbits and such things, and each household is also usually allowed a cow, a sow, and a limited number of sheep, goats, and bee-hives, though not many households would have all these. From these sources the family draws a good deal of its own food, but there is usually a surplus to take to market, and the Russian peasant is as tenacious as peasants anywhere else at extracting profit from small enterprises. These sales in the open market are perfectly legal; anything which the *kolkhoz* produces above its quota may be sold there too, and well-managed *kolkhozy* often add handsomely to their income in this way. In the towns there are buildings for the peasant markets; in the villages food is sold by the roadside, and any visitor to Russia can testify how prices are ruled by the law of supply and demand when peasants hawk their chickens, raspberries, melons, pastries, milk and so forth at the railway stations. The surprising thing is that the law of supply and demand is allowed to work freely in the markets as well. When government stores are full of clean, good-quality food the prices in the market fall; when, as in wartime, the government shops are nearly empty, the peasants may ask and get anything up to fifty times the normal price. At some periods the produce brought to market has amounted to as much as 30 per cent. of the whole agricultural produce of the U.S.S.R.; in 1960 41 per cent. of the meat, 47 per cent. of the milk, and 81 per cent. of the eggs in the Soviet Union still came from private producers.

The Communists dislike this survival of private trade, but they presumably feel that they could not afford to anger consumers by taking away their principal source of so many foods, and that the peasants must be allowed this safety-valve, or passive resistance might endanger the whole agricultural Plan. In practice many peasants seem to spend all or almost all their time on their own plots, and there is always the danger that grain, potatoes, etc., intended for the quota, may find their way illegally on to the open market where they usually fetch higher prices. The countryside is too big for continuous control to be possible, and one can read in the Soviet press of peasants or *kolkhoz* chairmen who have amassed large sums by arranging illegal deals, exchanges, and rackets of innumerable kinds. One can hardly be surprised at this, since the peasant's average cash income from the *kolkhoz* is about a third of that of the average wage-earner, though he also receives a good deal in kind. (He is taxed on his private earnings but not on his earnings from the *kolkhoz*.) In spite of the supply of simple clubs, libraries, schools, medical centres, etc., the peasant gets a poor share of the social services compared with the townsman. He is not paid when the *kolkhoz* is unable, perhaps owing to the weather, to provide him with work, while the wage-earner in similar circumstances is still entitled to his full pay. A peasant's pension is provided by the *kolkhoz* only, according to its ability, which may be very limited, while the town worker draws a state pension according to his wage. It is also not easy for the peasant to leave the land to take up other work.

Not far from half the population lives on this depressed scale in the 44,000 *kolkhozy*, though many improvements have been made under Khrushchev. It has proved impossible to apply dictatorship to the peasants in the same way as to the industrial workers, and one would imagine that better results would be got either by returning to individual farming organized in co-operatives, or by organizing the whole of the land in government farms. The first alternative would be unthinkable to Communists; the second is exactly what they would like to carry out. There has always been a small percentage of the land organized in state farms (*sovkhozy*); and farms devoted to special purposes such as seed-growing or horse-breeding are all of this kind. *Sovkhoz* workers are paid a regular wage and enjoy most of the other privileges of wage-earners. They also have plots of their own, but unless supervision is very bad they clearly cannot steal *sovkhoz* time to work on these. Before the war the *sovkhozy* comprised only 9 per cent. of the total 'sown area' in the U.S.S.R., but by 1959 the proportion had risen to 30 per cent., partly as a result of opening up the 'virgin lands'. *Kolkhozy* are also being pressed to join up in large associations for their own advantage, and in 1962 'agricultural directorates' were formed to administer farming over very large areas.

*Kolkhoz* farming is not a very remunerative form of agriculture, and the peasants' private production is obviously a very expensive method. It is no wonder that the average yield of Soviet agriculture, per head of persons employed, is only one-fourth or one-fifth that of the

United States, and this in spite of great extensions in grain; between 1954 and 1956 90 million virgin acres were brought into cultivation, and between 1953 and 1960 the total Soviet grain production is said to have increased by 62 per cent. The low general yield cannot entirely be blamed on organization, nor on climate or soil; insufficient fertilizers and poor quality of seed are also responsible. At the time of writing Mr. Khruschev's large-scale plans for fertilizer production and increased mechanization have been made to take second place to the further expanding of heavy industry and armaments, judged necessary by the Soviet leaders in their reading of the international situation. One may expect many more changes in Soviet agriculture before it reaches its goal (at present planned for 1970) of overtaking America.

To return to Soviet industry. When the First Five Year Plan was launched in 1928 it drew admiration from all over the world for its boldness and the way in which it was presented to the Soviet public. This was not quite the first time that a government had undertaken to catch up, in a generation or so, the industrial progress which other countries had achieved in a century or more. Japan was first in this respect, but Japan kept so much of her old social system that she did not inspire any other countries to follow her. In the U.S.S.R. a nation, for the first time in history, was shown through dramatic posters, graphs, and films the targets which it could reach if all did their part. (The very word 'target' hardly entered into the Western economist's vocabulary in those days.) Films about the Plan, such as *Turksib* or *The General Line*, remain among the classics of the cinema, and some of the posters remain classics of the art of publicity.

Enthusiasm, black bread, and cabbage were the principal articles of diet then. Life was extremely hard in the towns as well as in the collectivized countryside, but a great part of the Plan was in fact completed in four years, mainly through the ruthless policy of first things first, but also partly through the enthusiasm generated in the people. Tools were short but unskilled labour was plentiful, and youths and girls worked double shifts to make up for the lack of machinery and the scarcity even of hammers and screwdrivers. Technical skill was appallingly short, and many foreign technicians were given short-term contracts to work in the U.S.S.R. Organizing skill was appallingly short, too. It was a colossal task to impose habits of punctuality, self-discipline, neatness, and fore-thought upon the mass of workers recruited from the land. Many of those who should have imposed discipline were themselves undisciplined, and from top to bottom of the hierarchy it was too often felt that enthusiasm and undeviating loyalty to directives were all that was required. Consequently, the effects of ignorance and the general lack of order were only too often interpreted as sabotage. (Some acts of sabotage certainly were committed by people opposed to the Communist dictatorship.) When practical men protested that methods wouldn't work, they might easily be imprisoned as traitors, only to be released and rehabilitated later, perhaps, when events had proved them right. And yet the Plan succeeded in its main objectives—the provision of electric power and basic machinery.

The Second Five Year Plan (1933-37) was devoted largely to iron and steel and railroad transport, and brought some improvement in the standard of living. But in 1935 there began the terrible years of the purges, when no one, however conscientious and disciplined, was safe from arrest or execution, and as the writer Ehrenburg has since said, 'for any individual it was sheer luck that he survived'. The purges were probably ordered by Stalin in order to terrorize the whole country into submission in every way, and they had an important secondary aim, which was to provide several million labour camp workers for the most distant and uninhabitable regions of the U.S.S.R. It is well known how the Soviet armed forces suffered from the execution of some of their best leaders, such as Marshal Tukhachevsky, and men and women of all kinds of ability were lost to the country. (Most of the people arrested or executed in this period, high or low, have since been 'rehabilitated', and the labour camps have almost disappeared.) In 1940 a decree was passed which tied every worker to his job (though ways of evasion were still found by some), and this lasted until after Stalin's death. Even during the worst years, however, there were continuous and plentiful incentives other than fear. There were handsome bonuses and piecework rates for those who could earn them, and the record-breaking workers known as Stakhanovites were loaded with rewards and privileges. More often than not a Stakhanovite was not a man of exceptional brawn but someone who had invented a simple but ingenious way of increasing output. The norms set for the ordinary worker were frequently too high, so ways had to be found of getting round them; everyone—managers, foremen, and workers alike—was so hard pressed that, just as in tsarist days, a sort of tacit conspiracy against authority existed to make things tolerable.

The Third Plan was interrupted by the war, the grimmest and bloodiest in Russian history. Defeat was at times so near, and the losses so enormous, that it was not till sixteen years afterwards that facts were released from which the figure of twenty million dead could be estimated. And yet, to the surprise of many Soviet citizens, and against all the machines and organization of Nazi Germany, the Soviet armies won.

Post-war plans were at first concerned with reconstruction, in a period whose grimness was not properly appreciated abroad, owing to Stalin's censorship. Stalin died in 1953, and gradually there was relaxation both political and economic. The Sixth Plan, which should have occupied the years 1956-60, was found to be too ambitious. Soviet industry now had a firm basis for growth, but further growth obviously could not continue at the same spectacular rate as in the early days, when a 200 per cent. increase in production could be got by turning out quantities which were still small in comparison with the nation's needs. A slower rate of growth has now been accepted as natural, and the present Plan is a Seven Year Plan (1959-65). Heavy industry still gets the major share, but production of goods for the consumer has increased so enormously in the last few years that it would be almost impossible for the Government to fly in the face of public demand by seriously reducing the development of light industry. ('After forty years,' a Soviet journalist said to me—'after forty years of being told to work for posterity, at last we are being offered something in our hands *now*.') Attention is being given to industries previously neglected, such as the chemical industry (for plastics, artificial fibres, and fertilizers among other things); and now that the general tempo is easier, much more attention is being given to the defects, some of which are fantastic, in management and organization. Purges and labour camps have all but gone, but the government machine remains the same in essence, though it is worked with far more humanity and intelligence nowadays. The aftermath of Stalin's rule presents a rather confusing appearance, to which we shall return in the last chapter.

With all their ruthless priorities and senseless purges, their clumsiness and frequent failures, and all the cheating and chicanery which had to go on to make life barely tolerable, the early Five Year Plans saved the U.S.S.R. in the war. They had opened up new resources such as the iron of Magnitogorsk, huge coal deposits and copper mines in the Kazakhstan deserts, and new machine bases in the Kuznetsk and other districts of Western Siberia. It was to these bases, and others in the older industrial districts of the Urals, that so much factory equipment was evacuated from European Russia as the Germans advanced. Something of the achievement of Soviet industry through its whole existence is shown by the following figures, taken from the *Yearbook to the Soviet Encyclopædia* (1961):

| | 1913 | 1940 | 1953 | 1960 |
|---|---|---|---|---|
| Cast iron (millions of tons) | 4·2 | 14·9 | 27·4 | 46·8 |
| Steel      „      „      „ | 4·2 | 18·3 | 38·1 | 65·3 |
| Petroleum      „      „      „ | 9·2 | 31·1 | 52·8 | 148 |
| Electric power (million kilowatt hours) | 1,900 | 48,300 | 134,300 | 292,000 |
| Lorries and buses | — | 139,900 | 276,800 | 384,800 |
| Cars | — | 5,500 | 77,400 | 138,800 |
| Tractors, mechanical ploughs, &c. | — | 123,700 | 389,300 | 594,900 |
| Paper (million tons) | 0·2 | 0·8 | 1·61 | 2·4 |
| Cement „      „ | 1·5 | 5·7 | 16 | 45·5 |
| Bricks (millions) | 2,900 | 7,500 | 16,800 | 35,500 |
| Radio and TV sets | — | 160,000 | 1.72 m. | 5·9 m. |
| Refrigerators | — | 3,500 | 49,200 | 529,500 |
| Sewing machines | 270,000 | 170,000 | 990,000 | 3,096,000 |
| Knitted goods other than outerwear (million articles) | | 124·4 | 274·7 | 472·3 |
| Leather footwear (million pairs) | 60 | 211 | 238·1 | 419·3 |
| Woollen fabrics (million sq. metres) | 107·7 | — | 208·7 | 341·8 |

These figures of course do not show how far the increases are due to expansion and improvement of old bases, and how far to great new enterprises such as the Kuibyshev hydro-electric station—the largest in the world —or the new oilfields of the Urals and the Middle Volga, which now yield more than the traditional fields of Baku. Neither do such figures show the extent to which Plans have often been unfulfilled; in 1932, for instance, the

Second Plan set a target of 100 billion kilowatt-hours for the electrical industry by the end of the five years, but when 1937 arrived there was only 36 billion kwh. on tap. Even today industries may fall short by as much as 10 per cent. of fulfilling their plan, and in special fields, such as the design and manufacture of new machinery, by as much as 40 or 50 per cent., in some republics.

There is a great body of statistics about Soviet production nowadays, some of them quite detailed. It is a mistake to imagine that they are doctored for foreign consumption. During the war the Germans captured many tons of Soviet secret documents which later passed to the Allies; study of these has not shown any important discrepancy between figures published and figures circulated in confidential papers. The only difference seems to have been that unsatisfactory figures were often not made public until several years had elapsed. It is, however, important to examine Soviet statistics, like those of any other country, so as to be quite clear what they represent.[1] For

[1] This is particularly important when comparing Soviet statistics with those of other countries. For instance, Soviet expenditure on defence forms only one-sixth of the national budget, whereas in Britain the proportion is almost a quarter. But the Soviet ' budget ' includes not only such sums as are included in the British national budget, but also all the expenditure of local authorities and most of the capital investment in industry and agriculture, besides part of the working capital. To make a proper comparison between the two countries, therefore, we must add to the British national figure all the expenditure of local authorities raised from the rates, and comparable proportions of the investment and working capital of the whole of British privately-owned industry and agriculture. The result would show that Britain spends a smaller proportion of her national output on defence than the Soviet Union does. Again, the U.S.S.R. boasts of a death-rate of 7.2 per 1,000 compared with 9.3 per 1,000 in the U.S.A. But the U.S.A. has almost double the percentage of old people that the U.S.S.R. has; the ' crude death-rate ', as it is called, only appears to be higher for the same reason that the death-rate is high in healthy places such as Bournemouth, because so many elderly people go to spend their last years there. A proper comparison—what is called a weighted death-rate—would show a different result.

are also part of the plan, and each factory also contributes an estimate of its own potentialities. The director of each enterprise has complete authority in achieving his target, though he is subject to control commissions and inspectors, and he may be subject to complaint, or even in bad cases nowadays to dismissal, by the trade union of his workers, if he is not administering the wage fund or the social benefits according to the rules laid down. The union has no power to change the rules nor to demand a change of policy nor, of course, to modify the target figures. The director has no power to change these things either, and in Stalin's day if he failed to reach his target he and many of his staff could find themselves in labour camps or sentenced to be shot. Today he would suffer at most a fine, or a demotion, or a transfer to an unpleasant part of the country. On the other hand he has always had the incentive of a handsome bonus if he produces more than his quota.

The target rules all, and the director is responsible for fulfilling it while running his enterprise on a profit-and-loss basis. But where does he get his supplies? They are all part of the targets of perhaps a hundred other directors, some of them maybe many hundred miles away. If, for example, lubricating oil or leather belting run short, it may be little help for the director of the machine-tool factory to complain that the director of the oil mill or the leather factory has not filled his quota. In the early days he might have had to put some of his men to preparing oil from local resources. The director of the oil mill may be in a dilemma of his own; is it more important for him to supply the machine tool factory or to supply the construction plant of a new hydroelectric base to which he is also committed? The priorities multiply to the point where they can no longer be sorted out. In practice illegal methods are often resorted to. Bribes may pass, or leather example, motor-cars are counted in Soviet calculations as capital goods, whereas in Western countries they are consumption goods; milk in the U.S.S.R. may often be turned into butter to save it from spoiling before it reaches distant markets, but statistically it still counts as milk, so that the producers' milk quota may be fulfilled; housing space may or may not include such things as passageways; and in the general figures of production some things may appear more than once, as they pass through various stages. These are difficulties of a kind familiar to all students of statistics, and they are the chief reason why foreign economists put various interpretations upon the Soviet estimates of industrial progress. Many figures have never been published, but it was only during the last years of Stalin that large bodies of figures were distorted for reasons of policy (mostly internal). Since 1956 only certain figures are counted as state secrets, mainly those for non-ferrous metals and of course for military matters; there are also still few details to be had about the labour force in particular industries or jobs.

No one, remembering the defeat of the Nazis, can doubt that the Soviet Government were justified in building up their industrial and military strength so quickly. They ran the whole thing as though it were an operation of war, and there was probably no alternative to the policy of ruthless priorities. But it has left the economy very uneven in its development.

Communications, for one thing, are behindhand. The railway system is overloaded; about half of all the rail freight in the world is carried on the Soviet lines—at a cost of 55 railwaymen per mile, against $4\frac{1}{2}$ per mile in the U.S.A. The U.S.S.R. is better provided with railways than any part of the world outside Western Europe, North America, and India, and these cluster most thickly, of course, in the industrial regions. But elsewhere, and quite apart from the thinly inhabited North, there must be thousands of places in European Russia which are forty or fifty miles from a railway, and in Asia thousands which are still further away. Some of these places have the benefit of water transport, which in summer can be important over the great network of rivers and lakes, though services may be unpredictable owing to the great variation in water level between the spring floods and the late summer drought. Through communication between the White, Baltic, Black, and Caspian Seas was made possible, fairly early in the Soviet period, by the construction of the Moscow-Volga Canal, the Volga-Don Canal, and the Baltic-White Sea Canal (which was built with prison labour). There is a very good network of air services, particularly in districts which have little other transport, but what is terribly backward is road transport. Only one-sixth of the roads classed as main roads have a hard surface. There are a very few cross-country highways with such surfaces, and some shorter ones radiating from the largest cities, but the overwhelming majority of the country's roads are simply dirt tracks, impassable in the spring thaw and the rains of early autumn. To build modern roads and permanent bridges is difficult in a country with the climate of Russia; thousands of small timber bridges have to be dismantled every autumn to save them from the ice, and rebuilt again in spring. It is little wonder that only five per cent. of the nation's freight is carried by road.

Housing, and the public services connected with it, have also remained at a very low level. Russian peasant families have nearly always lived in single-room huts, and when they flooded into the towns they often found themselves more cramped than ever. To share a room with another family was commonplace, and it is only during the last few years that a great campaign of new construction has begun to relieve the whole desperate problem. In 1958 the average housing space per person was reckoned to be about 64 sq. ft. The Seven Year Plan envisages flats with about 500 sq. ft., including bathroom, kitchen, etc., for families of 3-5 persons. The annual output of new housing space has almost trebled in the last seven years, though even now housing materials can hardly be described as one of the highest priorities. Building is going on at the rate of over a million flats or dwellings a year, and people in the overcrowded Soviet cities are looking forward to relief in a not impossible future.

Public services have still very far to go; in 1960, out of 4,713 Soviet cities, 47 per cent. had no central drainage system, and 26 per cent. had no central water supply. Small towns and villages are even worse supplied. There are dwellings in Moscow itself without a proper water supply, and even in the pleasant-looking suburbs where better-off people live in wooden houses, water has often to be fetched over quite a distance from a tap or spring which is somehow kept unfrozen in winter.

Another result of the priority given to capital goods has been that goods for the ordinary consumer have been— and usually still are—poor in quality and design as well as in short supply. A Western visitor can easily be made sceptical by the contrast between the two kinds of manufacture. Perhaps they are all propaganda hoaxes—the sputniks and hydro-electric stations, the automatic production lines, the natural gas laid on from Saratov to Moscow, the giant draglines excavating the world's greatest reservoirs, and the machines 'to produce components accurate within 0.00025 mm. in size and roundness and having a "mirror" surface'. The ordinary visitor does not see a great deal of such things, but sees that the Soviet system is apparently unable (to quote the words of one of its own citizens) 'to organize the exits from a station properly ', or to produce clothes and domestic ornaments of more than (with a few exceptions) the clumsiest designs, or new housing where the concrete does not frequently become defective, or television sets more reliable than the present ones, of which between 60 per cent. and 70 per cent. (according to Soviet figures) have to go back for repair within six months of manufacture.

There is no hoax about the great achievements, though often there are not as many examples of the best of them as Soviet propaganda might like foreigners to believe. Soviet capital goods have been exported for many years to the countries of Asia, and some countries further west have found them useful too. But no Soviet propagandist would pretend that the emphasis has not been, until very recently, on capital rather than consumer goods. He would point, however, to the increases intended under the present Plan, for example:

### 1965 Production Targets

| Leather footwear | 515 m. pairs | = about 2.2 | |
| Cotton fabrics | 5,700 m. sq. metres | = about 24.7 | per head of the population |
| Fabrics of wool or artificial wool | 635 m. sq. metres | = about 2.7 | |
| Fabrics of silk and other artificial fibres | 1,218 m. sq. metres | = about 5.3 | |
| Hosiery | 1,250 m. pairs | = about 5.4 | |

These are all well below the American production figures, except for wool, but they represent increases of 25 to 50 per cent. over the seven years. The gross output of all light industry is planned to increase by about 50 per cent. between 1959 and 1965.

There are continuous complaints from the public, and in the Soviet press, about the shortages and the quality, design, and facilities for repair and maintenance of almost everything which the individual consumer needs. A few manufactured articles, such as cameras and watches, have reached a good standard, but cameras and watches need only be made to a few patterns; they do not need to be tailored to the individual customer, nor do they often require spares.

The fact is that the capital goods industries have absorbed until recently the best of the country's organizing and designing talent; the Plans were organized that way, and many Soviet citizens still regard it as socially inferior to work at manufacture for the retail market, or still more to engage in such trivial professions as serving in a shop, cutting people's hair, or working as a cook. There are far from enough shops, particularly in the countryside, and some kinds of service, such as house-painting or small repair jobs, are extremely hard to get.

It may not have been too difficult, after the first crude beginnings, for the Plans to organize labour, materials, and skill for the construction of machine tools, combine harvesters, diesel engines, etc., and to see that they were delivered where they were needed; it has proved very much more difficult to organize the production of several hundred types of dress or shoe, a dozen kinds of soap or sugar or saucepan, and to get these to the tens of thousands of selling points where they are needed.

These are difficulties peculiar to the production of consumer goods in the U.S.S.R. But there are also serious difficulties which arise from the way in which planning has been organized in general. The principle is simple. A national target figure is agreed for, say, the production of machine tools, and it is broken down into sub-targets for the various areas of the country and finally into target figures for each enterprise, of which there are nowadays 200,000 (for all kinds of manufacture) in the U.S.S.R. The plans are not altogether arbitrary; they have to be adjusted to the materials and manpower available, which are also part of the plan, and each factory also contributes an estimate of its own potentialities. The director of each enterprise has complete authority in achieving his target, though he is subject to control commissions and inspectors, and he may be subject to complaint, or even in bad cases nowadays to dismissal, by the trade union of his workers, if he is not administering the wage fund or the social benefits according to the rules laid down. The union has no power to change the rules nor to demand a change of policy nor, of course, to modify the target figures. The director has no power to change these things either, and in Stalin's day if he failed to reach his target he and many of his staff could find themselves in labour camps or sentenced to be shot. Today he would suffer at most a fine, or a demotion, or a transfer to an unpleasant part of the country. On the other hand he has always had the incentive of a handsome bonus if he produces more than his quota.

The target rules all, and the director is responsible for fulfilling it while running his enterprise on a profit-and-loss basis. But where does he get his supplies? They are all part of the targets of perhaps a hundred other directors, some of them maybe many hundred miles away. If, for example, lubricating oil or leather belting run short, it may be little help for the director of the machine-tool factory to complain that the director of the oil mill or the leather factory has not filled his quota. In the early days he might have had to put some of his men to preparing oil from local resources. The director of the oil mill may be in a dilemma of his own; is it more important for him to supply the machine tool factory or to supply the construction plant of a new hydroelectric base to which he is also committed? The priorities multiply to the point where they can no longer be sorted out. In practice illegal methods are often resorted to. Bribes may pass, or leather might be bought on the open market (almost certainly from an illegal source) at a high price which the director would hope to recoup by economies elsewhere. Exchanges often take place, and there is quite a class of person, called a *tolkach* or fixer, who makes a good living out of the commission gained by putting a factory with a surplus in touch with another which is short. There are innumerable accounts of this sort of thing in the Soviet press, and the main business of lawyers in the U.S.S.R. appears to be to deal, perhaps at a stage after the target has been reached, with the suits brought by one enterprise or corporation against another which let them down.

In 1957 it was felt that the concentration of so much authority in Moscow made these breakdowns, delays, and illegal practices almost impossible to control. Most of the country's industry was transferred from the control of the central ministries to a new form of regional economic organization, called a *sovnarkhoz*. There are now about 40 of these, and each is responsible for most of the industry, whether heavy or light, and the building, within its own area. Transport remains under centralized or republican control, besides the industries connected with defence and the chemical industry (which has been very backward). The *sovnarkhozy* now turn out 71 per cent. of Soviet production, but they are not concerned with retail trade; that also is under republican control. To allow each *sovnarkhoz* to organize the sale of its own products would, at least in present circumstances, be putting far too much temptation in the way of managers; there is already too much illegal selling of surpluses or of small quantities filched from stock. Directors of enterprises are often responsible, especially in less developed districts, for the housing of their workers, for child nurseries, canteens, and even retail shops. Some directors, it seems, make a good thing out of such sidelines, and some develop subsidiary industries of their own, like the managerial staff of an ironworks in the Kursk region, who were eventually brought to court for misappropriating two million bricks, with which they built forty-seven houses, some of which they sold to their friends.

The national plan is still broken up into republican plans and then passed on to the *sovnarkhozy*, but the new organizations have more freedom within their own areas. To continue the example above, a *sovnarkhoz* would usually control the production of machine tools and lubricating oil and leather belting, as well as almost every other sort of production, in its region. There is also some small-scale production organized by local soviets of simple articles, such as pots, from local materials.

The greater freedom which is now possible in carrying out the Plan has naturally brought new problems; there might be a reversion—probably temporary—to firmer central control, or there might be freer developments, under the new managerial generation, of a kind not yet seen. In spite of all the difficulties and even absurdities which arise under the Plans, it should not be forgotten that they have much more often been fulfilled (or over-fulfilled) than not.

There are a number of advantages in the Soviet system. Investment can be concentrated where it is most needed, instead of where it is likely to bring in the best short-term profits. Only a dictatorial system, in all probability, combined with state ownership, could have kept the national belt so fiercely tightened for many years, with the phenomenal growth of heavy industry as a result. Soviet enterprises all belong to the state (though they may be administered by a great many intermediate bodies); they have no rent to pay and no interest on their capital investments, only depreciation. Their working capital is borrowed from one of the state banks at two per cent. interest, or it may come from their own profits. Government finance comes mainly from a simple turnover tax on most kinds of industrial production, which is of course passed on to the consumer in the prices which he has to pay. As supplies increase, prices are usually lowered, but some things, such as vodka, may be kept artificially dear in order to discourage consumption. Many other taxes, such as the tax on peasant sales, are imposed for political rather than financial reasons; the turnover tax contributed about 41 per cent. of the national budget in 1960, and another 26 per cent. came from a tax on the profits of enterprises. Income tax is in process of being abolished—it was never very high—and it is proposed before long to introduce some free services, perhaps for local transport. But these advantages are of course no more than a convenience; the revenue which formerly arose from income tax or bus fares has to come out of the prices paid by the consumer for other things.

The main economic weaknesses of the Soviet system are three: there is no adequate way of calculating costs or prices; there is insufficient machinery for discovering what the consumers want or need; and the system of quotas is not sufficiently broken down into what is called 'assortment'. (A quota can often be fulfilled by producing mainly the articles which are cheapest or easiest to manufacture, and few of the others.) It would be too facile to assume that such difficulties can never be overcome under a system of public ownership; some attempts are being made in the U.S.S.R., in spite of the dead hand of a good deal of doctrine and vested Party interest, and in Yugoslavia each enterprise, although state-owned, more or less decides its own output and fixes its own prices more or less according to the market.

How does the ordinary citizen come off under the system today? His standard of living has risen a good deal in the last few years; there is much more to buy, and prices on the whole have fallen since the war, though a Soviet citizen still has to work longer than an Englishman or American in order to earn the prices of almost any article, whether basic necessity or luxury. If we take a Soviet worker on a good average wage, equivalent by its middle position in the salary scale, though not in purchasing power, to £14 or £15 a week in England, he might have to work, at the time of writing, four times as long as the Englishman to buy a pound of butter, $2\frac{1}{2}$ times as long to buy a pound of the cheapest meat, $2\frac{1}{2}$ times as long for a cheap T.V. set, and three times as long for the cheapest make of car. The Russian would be extremely lucky to be able to buy a car, in any case; the waiting list is at least two years long. What he probably wants more than anything else is one of the new flats, and when he has got the flat, some furniture to put in it. For these he may also have to wait several years; meanwhile his wife finds an increasing variety of clothes in the shops, and if she tries again and again and uses some under-the-counter methods, she will, in time, get more or less the outfit she wants. She is not likely to be too hard to please; it is not many years since she had no hope of getting even her own size of shoes or gloves or skirt, let alone a design she might like.

Meanwhile the rent they have to pay is very low, usually less than seven per cent. of their income, and when they get a new flat it will still be low. They may be one of the fortunate families who also have a *dacha* or country shack, hardly more perhaps than a large summerhouse, which they may be able to rent from its owner, or they may have to save for three or four years in order to buy one.

They work—both of them, probably—a forty-one hour week, finishing at about 3.0 p.m. on Saturday. They probably have three weeks' paid holiday, or if they are skilled or professional workers four, five, or even six weeks. They have no fear of unemployment; on the contrary, if they are observed by authority not to be employed, they may find themselves urged into uncongenial jobs. While they are at work they may well be less bored than workers in many other countries: they are much more involved with their fellow workers because there are nearly always more people working on a given job in the U.S.S.R. than in Britain; according to a recent issue of *Pravda* 47 per cent. of Soviet workers have no mechanical aids. For a Russian, too, the wall newspaper with its news of individual and group successes or failures, the Honours Board for the best workers, and the constant 'socialist competition' between different units are all in keeping with the national character; they engender enthusiasm in more people; cynicism in fewer, than would be natural in Britain.

When a Soviet worker falls ill he is entitled to sick pay varying from 50 per cent. to 90 per cent. of his salary, according to his length of service, provided he has been at least six months in the same job, and provided also that he is a member of his trade union, as most people are. (Non-members get only half the benefits.) Health services are free (except for medicines at the pharmacists), and the official figures show that there is one doctor to every 570 persons, and by 1965 there should be one to every 460, while there are already 7 hospital beds per thousand of the population. Diseases such as cholera, typhus, malaria, plague, and trachoma have been all but wiped out.

A man can retire from work at the age of 60, a woman at 55, and they draw pensions based on their earnings—the lower the earnings the higher the percentage of pension up to a maximum pension of 120 roubles a month, which is a very fair middle-bracket income on Soviet standards. The pensionable age is low because people age quickly in the U.S.S.R., owing to the extremely hard lives they have had to lead until very recently, but one may expect the age to be raised in the future. No contributions are payable for either pensions or health services, and pension payments are supposed to be brought to the pensioner's door by the postman. Great numbers actually continue working after 60 and people are often pressed to do so.

Finally there is the education system, which is of course free and is highly regarded. Full-time education is compulsory only between the ages of seven and fifteen, and in some country districts some children probably get no more. Elsewhere, however, a large proportion of children attend a 'ten-year school' which takes them up to 17, with something like the same subjects as in a small English grammar school. Children have the same school building, the same teachers, and the same equipment throughout the 10 years; there is no separation at 11 or any other age in these schools. But a great many children are in fact separated, because they leave the eight-year schools at 15 and enter either a vocational school with a one-to-three year course, or a 'technicum' with a three-year course (a technical school which also takes older students). It is always denied that there is any test to decide the type of school a child should attend after 15; the parents' choice is said to be free. This has often meant that too many parents have chosen the ten-year school, with the result that at the age of 17 their children have not wanted to take up manual employment, in spite of various campaigns to recommend it. The ten-year school is therefore being made into an eleven-year school (i.e. up to the age of 18) and, for some years past, pupils in their last three or four years have been supposed to 'engage in productive work' for a part of the school week. How far children have been fitted into local factories and enterprises, and how productive the work may have been, it is difficult to say. Further, if a young person who has finished the ten-year school wishes to go to the university (assuming he or she has high enough marks from school), then two years' work (at normal wages) in some kind of job 'related to one's ultimate speciality' is compulsory first. The top Soviet scientists have recently protested that because of this method, and the all-pervading refusal to acknowledge that some children are brighter than others, it is becoming difficult to get students who will make good scientists.

The U.S.S.R. is certainly turning out a much higher proportion of qualified mathematicians, physicists, engineers, and especially technicians than we are in Britain, but this fact should not blind us to some of the other features of Soviet education. The teaching is usually formal, consisting largely of rote-learning, there is little choice of textbook or of subject, and many higher courses are to our way of thinking much too specialized. (History for the school-leaving examination is Russian and Soviet history only.) A pupil who has studied a foreign language in the ten-year school for several years often has no better knowledge of it than someone with a poor O-level pass in Britain; not uncommonly his knowledge is less. The final examinations in Soviet schools and universities are mostly oral, they consist of few questions, and if a candidate is unable to answer one of them he is allowed to ask for another. School examinations are not conducted by public bodies or universities but by local bodies consisting of teachers from the school and probably people from the local education authority. The Russians with their deep-rooted (and certainly good-natured) feeling for equality seem to shy away from the idea of separating children according to their abilities. But school work is taken much more seriously than in England by children, parents, and teachers, and there can be pressure *from one's own school-fellows*, as well as one's elders, to improve on one's bad marks. This works very well in the Russian atmosphere, and in spite of the formality and comparative narrowness children seem to love school, teachers (although not well paid) are much respected, and parents' associations are usually active. It is a great feat to have built up such an education system in a short time, and Soviet citizens are proud of it.

This outline of the social services leaves out, I fear, a great deal of the reality—the queueing for chits, the stuttering halts in procedure, the schools so overcrowded that they work double or treble shifts, the ' rest homes ' with beds packed tightly side by side, and running through everything the lack of responsible administrative commonsense at lower levels, which makes so much of life a weariness in the U.S.S.R.

The Soviet citizen is used to this as he is used to the endless difficulties of shopping and transport, or as he is used, for example, to the censorship. He is quite able to read between the lines of his newspapers, dull as they are; he often suspects that people in Western countries are in many ways better off than he is; he yawns at the monotony and dullness of so much life in the U.S.S.R.—but it is all a great deal better than the famines of the early nineteen-twenties, the semi-starvation of the early nineteen-thirties, the insane police terror of Stalin's days, or the misery and horror of the war. (Those who are too young to have known these may have different reactions, of which something will be said in the next chapter.) You could get your Soviet citizen to complain about a hundred details of everyday life, or even about officialdom in general, and perhaps he might comment on the unfairness of collective farm life for the peasants. But only a few more original spirits would be willing to consider the whole economic, political, and social setting of their lives as 'the system', in the way in which simple Western propagandists so often see it.

I have left the political picture to the end of this chapter because, although it is easy to say what the organization is supposed to be on paper, it is extremely difficult to say exactly how it works in practice; even a group of well-placed Soviet officials, if one could divest them of all Party or national prejudice, would probably disagree about what actually goes on and would have to admit to a good deal of ignorance. On the other hand the purpose of the political organization—to bring about economic and social changes through the dictatorship of the Communist leaders—is clear enough, and I thought it logical to describe that purpose and its results first.

There is in the U.S.S.R. a hierarchy of councils or soviets elected by the people, starting with the village and district (*raion*) soviets, through city and provincial (*oblast*) soviets, up to Soviets of the Republics and the Supreme Soviet, which is officially the governing body of the whole U.S.S.R. The Supreme Soviet consists of the Soviet of the Union, on the basis of one member to every 300,000 inhabitants, and the Soviet of Nationalities, which exists for the purpose which its name implies.

Laws are not laws until approved by the Supreme Soviet, just as in Britain they are not laws until approved and signed by the Queen. Like the Queen, the Supreme Soviet never refuses consent. The Supreme Soviet meets for only a few days in the year, for ratifying and propaganda purposes and minor discussion, but many of its members sit on the permanent commissions which do some of the work, such as the drafting of new laws, which is done by civil servants in other countries.

Soviets of lesser rank likewise indulge in little discussion, but they do carry out many of the same functions as county, town, or village councils elsewhere; they are responsible locally for housing, roads, street lighting, transport, etc. The local medical officers, borough engineers, and such officials are usually members of their soviet, and this underlines the fact that local soviets are much more like bodies of local government servants than the councils which we know; it is not thought peculiar that the functions of taking decisions and carrying them out should be mixed up together. Local soviets can show a good deal of initiative, if they wish, but they are always limited by the fact that their revenues are allotted to them as part of the State Budget. Neither the local soviets nor the Supreme Soviet are elected to carry out particular policies, because in the sense in which we understand the word they are not elected at all. There is only one policy—that of the Communists and what are called their 'non-party sympathizers'; and any attempt at organizing another policy or faction, even in the smallest way, would still be hunted down and suppressed as sharply as in the past. There are no parties to contest the elections, which are supposed to take place in order to elect the best men and women, as individuals, for the job. But the voters are not even allowed the choice between one person and another—perhaps because a choice between persons might easily become a choice between policies. Contested public elections in the U.S.S.R., apart perhaps from a few freak instances, are unknown. Elections are a propaganda occasion, when one ' votes '—and one is indeed almost obliged to ' vote '— in order to register approval of official policy. One does

---

7. (a) *Karl Marx* (1818-1883).
   (b) *Lenin* (1870-1924).
   (c) *Stalin* (died 1953).
   (d) *N. S. Khrushchev*, President of the Council of Ministers of the U.S.S.R.
8. *A Typical Family Room.*

8

not even need a residential qualification in order to vote. The candidates are often chosen, indeed they are supposed always to be chosen, by a process of filtering possible names through trade union branches, factory organizations, and Communist Party branches, all of which are empowered to submit candidates for the eventual nomination. The process takes place under the watchful eye of Party officials, and it does result in the election of some public-spirited and morally sound people, though they must all follow the same policy.

For in the U.S.S.R. government is effectively carried out by the Communist Party. The Party is the organizing force and governmental élite, the focus of all political organization and ideas, and also the source of attitudes (broadly speaking) concerning morals, the arts, and all social questions. Its membership is at present about 9 millions[1], or $4\frac{1}{2}$ per cent. of the population. One cannot join the Party by merely paying a subscription and declaring support for its policies, as one does with a Western political party. One is not wanted in it as a mere supporter, though the mass of the population are encouraged to be 'non-party sympathizers'. The Party is bound to remain comparatively small, because the only people wanted are, roughly speaking, the born organizing secretaries, scout masters, propagandists, etc. You are only wanted if you are willing to give up your spare time and energy to controlling and organizing duties, and to indulging above all in what is called 'agitation', which means getting support for government measures among the people you mix

[1] The youth organization or *Komsomol* has 18 million members and the Pioneers, for children of 9 to 14, has 19 million. Young people are indoctrinated in these organizations, but they also go in for the same sort of activities as scouts and guides and youth clubs in other countries. The purpose of the Pioneers and the *Komsomol* is to ensure that none but Communist influence is allowed to run young people's organizations, rather than to train all the 37 million as Party members.

with. In short, the Communist Party is not a political party in our sense, but a directing and organizing élite. All this does not prevent some of the best people in the U.S.S.R. from being Party members; they are often pressed to join, because of their popularity, and for anyone who feels a sense of political duty there is no other organization which he can join. But the full-time officials in general are not popular. Once a member of the Party you cannot resign, though you may be expelled. It is your duty to form a ' cell ' (with a minimum of two other members) in every organization or community in which you may be involved. Thus there are Party units not only for geographical or administrative divisions of the country, but also in every soviet, every factory or other enterprise, trade union branch, club, school staffroom, theatre company, editorial office and so on. In theory, at least, there are such units, for even Communist devotion can become spread very thin at the lower levels. In practice the Party members may be the managers or leaders of an organization, or they may hold apparently unimportant positions; it is not usually difficult to recognize them for what they are. In 1962 the Party was reorganized into two separate divisions: one for agriculture from the highest to the lowest level, the other for industry.

Even the nine million members of the Party are not organized on what we would call democratic lines. They elect their own officers in each branch, and it is supposed to be a serious offence to impose officers from above, though in the more important posts careful ' vetting ' and other methods mean that this is more or less what happens. Discussion inside Party units is limited by the rules; one may disagree in the course of discussion, but taking a steady line of opposition, or forming a faction, is forbidden. The new Party programme adopted in 1961 says: ' The broadest democracy must go hand in hand with strict observance of comradely discipline ', which might be interpreted in Western terms somewhat as follows: 'All members must have the policy fully explained to them and must be brought to discuss any doubts and reservations so that these can be got rid of without members feeling they have been dictated to. But in order to make the Party an efficient organization everyone must accept discipline, though they should accept it of their own free will, and rather as an expression of the common will than as something imposed from above.' ('Democracy' in Communist terminology means government for the people rather than government by the people.)

The Party elects a Central Committee of between 100 and 200 members, which is an important training ground for members of the Presidium, a body of twenty or so top members including such well-known figures as Messrs. Khrushchev, Mikoyan, Suslov, and Kozlov. This is the real governing body and in effect *the only policy-making body* in the country. How much disagreement goes on inside the Presidium we do not know, but its results can often be seen in changes of policy or changes of personnel at the next lower level. The executive arm is the Council of Ministers, whose Chairman, or prime minister, is at present Mr. Khrushchev. Ministers are highly responsible people, and top Party leaders are very often important Ministers as well. At this level there is thus something of the same link between executive and legislature as there is in the dual functions of the members of the British Cabinet, except that neither executive nor legislature, in the U.S.S.R., is accountable to the elected representatives of the people. The Council of Ministers is the busiest and most important body in the land; it issues countless orders and decrees, without waiting for action or ratification by the Supreme Soviet, and far beyond the utmost scope of the British civil servant's Orders in Council. Committees attached to the Council of Ministers (and appointed, like the Ministers, by the highest Party authority) are in charge of very important jobs such as State Planning, State Security, the supervision of the arts and of religious matters.

Yet all this government by the Party does not mean, as is often supposed by foreigners, that everything is done by simply handing down orders as in the armed forces, with penalties for disobedience or failure at every stage. The business of a country is far too complicated for this to be possible, the distances in the U.S.S.R. are often too great, and there must be other incentives besides fear which will encourage people to hand the orders down. Control can never be complete, and the more it is insisted on, the more people will invent ingenious ways of circumventing it; an encyclopædia of these could be compiled from the Soviet press. Communist leadership, like that of every other country, does have to take some account of public reactions, as for example when the collectivization was modified and the peasants were granted their personal plots. Politics is only the art of the possible, under Communist dictatorship as everywhere else, and this implies, at various levels and to a certain extent, the cooperation and even initiative of the people who are governed. The Communist authorities are constantly calling for more initiative—that is, initiative in carrying out the policies—but most people have been too frightened by police control in the past, or too dulled by the narrowness of their job, or inhibited by the formality of their education, or held back by their own unspoken group loyalties, to be able to show much of the initiative required. However, at the level of everyday life a great deal more initiative is nowadays being shown and permitted.

But even if all citizens were to become miraculously enthusiastic, perfectly intelligent toilers for the Party line, there are always groups whose interests demand special policy or clash with the interests of other groups. And since there is no proper way in which discussion can take place inside the Party, the inevitable pressures by, for example, the new managerial class, the police, the peasants, or the intelligentsia have to proceed by secret intrigues among leaders. And the real differences inside the Presidium itself may have to be fought out secretly, by such methods as Mr. Khrushchev used when he influenced the appointment of Party chiefs all over the country, so that the Presidium was eventually faced with a new Central Committee of whom a majority backed Mr. Khrushchev and his policies, and were prepared if need be to elect a new Presidium. But all this goes on necessarily behind the scenes. No one knows the full story at any one moment, though most of it may come out later, and lower down the scale it is often true that no one is sure how rules are to be interpreted. Thus a foreigner may meet one official who astonishes him by his liberal interpretation of a regulation, and another who interprets it in a painfully strict and wooden way; the second, just as likely as the first, may be the man who is out of touch with the real intentions of the policy-makers. Intentions are often allowed to filter down without formal orders being made public; for example, the old decree which tied people to their jobs was gradually allowed after Stalin's death to become a dead letter, before it was repealed in 1956. No announcement was ever made—perhaps it was thought to show too dangerously sharp a turn of policy— about the closing of the labour camps which went on for several years, yet before long everyone had met some long-lost friend who had returned and was being rehabilitated. The power of the political police is only a fraction of what it was—arbitrary arrest is very little feared now—but people do not know, because they are not meant to, how far the spying and the reports of the police and their agents may still reach.

So the Soviet citizen has become skilled at interpreting trends, at following the ups and downs of people listed at Kremlin receptions, and above all at knowing which official, out of several possible, is the key man to approach in a given situation.

All this vagueness and uncertainty, with the inefficiency which it causes, is due of course to the lack of any proper outlet for expressing opposition or difference of opinion. Naturally the leadership would like to get rid of the inefficiency, and they have encouraged some comparatively liberal developments at lower levels which will be described in the next chapter. Meanwhile the population at large have more use than ever of the one safety-valve which has always been theirs—the liberty to express criticism or complaint openly, in the wall newspaper, in the ordinary newspaper, through their trade unions, or by writing to their representative in the Supreme Soviet,[1] and so on, *when policy has not been carried out*—whether in the shape of goods in the local shop, the service of local transport or telephones, the withholding of privileges, unjustified dismissal, or a short pay packet. If one is in a humble position it may be unwise to complain about one's superiors, and yet it is clear, from many reports in the press and cases in the courts, that people do manage to get a number of wrongs righted. One may have to go the local Party organization with one's complaint, and here the key personnel may often be, in their ordinary capacities, the very managers or local soviet officials about whom

[1] One of the principal responsibilities of deputies is to take up complaints of this kind from constituents.

one wishes to complain. However, higher Party authority takes a serious view of the hushing up of complaints, and local Party organizations have often been brought to book, through one channel of complaint or another, for injustices they have committed or condoned.

# 4

## TODAY AND TOMORROW

THE U.S.S.R. IS in a state of transition from grim Stalinist Communism to some other kind of society which is not easy to foresee, and for which there is probably no historical precedent.

There will at least be no turning back from a socialist economy to any kind of capitalism. No informed foreign observer would suggest that this might happen, and even Soviet refugees are hardly ever in favour of it, though they have much to criticize in the socialist economy, particularly in agriculture, whose organization is one of the biggest question marks in the Soviet future.

Apart from this, however, Marxist principles do not seem much of a guide to what is to come, since for the last forty years the major developments in the U.S.S.R. have so often taken place under the pressure of necessity and Marxist theory has been adapted so as to 'explain' them later.

Soviet citizens date the relaxation they now enjoy from the Twentieth Congress of the Communist Party in 1956. This was the occasion when Mr. Khrushchev in a private session denounced Stalin and the abuses of his reign. Reports of this speech were not published, but were allowed to filter slowly among the people, in case unrest should be caused by too sudden a turnabout. Even now it is usual to speak of 'the period of the cult of personality' rather than to use Stalin's name when condemning old abuses and tyrannies. (To reject Stalin entirely would have looked dangerously like rejecting Communism.) Before the Congress the labour camps had begun to release their prisoners, and the people had begun to realize that the powers of the security police were to be curbed. Khrushchev's speech convinced the public that they had little to fear in future from arbitrary arrest, and the implied promise has been kept. It would still be easy to get arrested for trying to form opposition groups, but Soviet citizens rarely try to do this. The Congress established that it was now permissible to criticize the practical details and execution of policy as well as the persons engaged in it, up to a very high level. The national machine badly needed this kind of relaxation, and it has of course been a great relief to the public. Six years later the *Literary Gazette* said the Twentieth Congress 'had put an end to the policy of beating out economic success at any price', and most Soviet citizens would probably agree.

The Government clearly feels more confident of its standing with the people nowadays. Stalin was hardly ever seen in public, and never without a large bodyguard, while Mr. Khrushchev and his associates go about in open cars and mix with the people as informally as an American President. There are far fewer slogans and portraits of leaders in the streets than there used to be; Soviet television—a comparatively new service—is less burdened with propaganda than the radio is; the leadership feels secure enough to allow a mention now, in war books, of the demoralization and panic which occurred in 1941 as the Germans advanced; and in 1960 a Moscow newspaper was allowed to publish the results of a poll taken among 1,400 Muscovites—a kind of social document previously unheard of in Russia: 73 per cent. of those questioned said their standard of living had improved in recent years (i.e. 27 per cent. thought that their standard had not!), and when asked what was their most urgent personal problem, half the people said 'housing' as might have been expected, but 27 per cent. dared to say 'higher wages'.

Along with the political relaxation the Soviet people found a new policy on consumer goods. Between 1955 and 1959, while retail prices remained stable, retail trade increased (according to a German estimate) by 45 per cent., and retail trade no longer meant mainly food. There are not merely more clothes and household articles in the shops; there is more variety and better quality, though still nothing like the variety and quality which people want. In the cities Russian people, whom superficial observers ten years ago dismissed as glum and austere, are now queueing for luxury articles. The Government newspaper, *Izvestia*, says it is wrong that nylons, black lingerie, and frilly underwear should be in such short supply. Clumsy, crudely-designed articles are being left in the shops, and the press attacks the factories and the designers —still very much in the majority—who are responsible for these. There are fairly large imports of better-class consumer goods from the satellite countries, and the Government even allows for the first time a trickle of foreign luxury imports, such as good English knitted goods, cosmetics, and some of the best makes of china.

Through all these changes the Soviet people have naturally become more relaxed in their ways. There is no longer, for example, the same national urgency to work overtime, and in fact overtime is generally discouraged. Social habits are becoming more sophisticated. Young people may nowadays be seen kissing or holding hands in the parks—discreetly indeed, but in the old days this would have been quite unthinkable, 'un-Russian'. Kisses on the cinema screen are also now permissible; the first film to be so abandoned as to show a true love-kiss caused a sensation.

People are taking life more easily and even lazily. In the new blocks of flats, for the first time in Russian history, thousands of modest-income families are able to lock the door of their apartment against the outside world and bring up their children in the affection and indulgence of an isolated home. The good nature which children used to feel, in the old days of overcrowding, from a score of neighbouring 'uncles' and 'aunts', is now more concentrated in the person of their parents. Parents do not want their children to have such a hard time as they knew themselves, and some of them indulge their children too much, so that spoiled youths and girls, and consequential delinquency, are now quite a Soviet social problem.

Soviet socialist progress has in many ways bred more individuality and opportunities for individuality than ever existed in Tsarist Russia. The spread of education, industry, science, and the arts has opened up a thousand careers instead of the few poor possibilities of the old Russian village. New dwellings, new clothes, and new attainments are inevitably breeding more individual pride, and the old Russian communal feeling is nothing like so strong as it was. No wonder that the Government uses so many methods—often naïve to our way of thinking—in order to remind citizens that they are all members of one great community, working for each other and not for themselves. And yet the Government also calls for 'individuals', for 'initiative', for people who will take the lead in the virgin lands or the Arctic, in breaking down bottlenecks in production, rooting out abuses, getting rid of red tape, improving service to the consumer, and so on.

The enthusiasm of some of the best people in the U.S.S.R. is indeed captured by such appeals. But other people have such an inheritance of dictatorship and red tape, and they can feel so impotent under the contradictions of Soviet life, the rigidity on paper and the uncertainty in practice, that they can fall—as one may read in the Soviet press—into apathy, laziness, cynicism, and self-seeking. Russians are not naturally good at self-discipline, and they have not had much encouragement to breed the real self-discipline which comes from within.

The new opportunities have created a great class, numbered at twenty-two million persons in 1961—the vastly enlarged *intelligentsia*, which in Soviet Russian means simply brain workers, from clerk up to professor. The lower grades earn less than the best-paid manual workers, but a great many of the intelligentsia earn more, and they almost all lead easier lives and are rather envied. The Government is now narrowing the difference between the highest salaries and the lowest, and puts out much propaganda to encourage more people to take up manual work. (Some highly-qualified persons with a 20,000 rouble salary have had it cut by half.) The persons most respected and admired are not the leaders of policy and administration (the Government itself does not publicise these people, apart from the members of the Presidium); they are those individuals who are most individual—the leading dancers, actors, writers, musicians, artists, architects, engineers, professors, and pioneers of all kinds, and they are admired for their talents and achievements, rather than for the comparatively privileged lives they lead. They might be called in Western terms the leaders of Soviet society. But at somewhat lower levels, especially in administration, there are many comfortable niches which are sought after by people who want an easy life.

The most recent policy is aimed at reducing the number of these parasites, by drawing more and more of the people into voluntary administration: 'An effort should be made to ensure that the salaried government staffs are reduced, and that work on government staffs should eventually cease to constitute a profession'. Comrades' Courts now exist, based on a work unit or a residential unit, where unpaid, elected members have jurisdiction in lesser offences. In Soviet cities one sees the red armbands of the *Druzhina,* or 'Company' of voluntary guardians of public order and manners, who work by persuasion rather than by threats. And in the local soviets members are now taking much more part in the work of actually organizing and supervising schools, building, health services, etc.

These new devices are rather in line with Russian traditions, but they may not altogether succeed, or they may succeed only by drawing more and more people into the Party machine. For the old framework of control indubitably remains. It would still be possible, with very little change in the machine, to return to the days of draconian discipline and arbitrary arrest. It would still be possible for a ruthless leader, over a long period, to exploit the system of government for his own ends until he became another Stalin. Such reversions are very unlikely, because the whole weight of popular feeling and the trend of recent policy are against them, but they are not impossible. The U.S.S.R. is full of contradictions today, and the attitudes of the Government must often remain ambivalent too. The stick is kept in reserve as well as the carrot; control can be subtly exercized, and then some severe little measure will give the people a sharp reminder that power does not ultimately rest with them. Death sentences are suddenly passed on speculators, to serve as a warning to others. The growth of privately-owned *dachas* is curbed by a decree to divert private savings into 'co-operative building of new blocks'. At the elections for the Supreme Soviet in 1962 the 'preliminary' results showed that more people than ever before—about 1,200,000—had voted against the official candidates; the 'final' results, instead of confirming the earlier trend as usual, were quietly amended to a less disturbing total. Religion is not persecuted so directly as in the early days, but several thousand churches are reckoned to have been quietly closed during the last few years, with no flourish of anti-religious trumpets. And satire, social pressures, and discriminatory measures are used against the Church, the priests, and Soviet church-goers, especially the young, who are not uncommonly attracted by the Russian Church, if only because it is something which is not in the least 'Soviet'. More foreign books and periodicals reach the U.S.S.R. than used to be the case, but they are not always allowed a free passage, they are accessible only to special classes of reader, and even scientific journals may arrive with passages deleted which reflect distantly and vaguely against Soviet policy, or which show other countries in too favourable a political light. Most Soviet citizens will nowadays talk readily to foreigners, yet if they pursue a foreign acquaintanceship or correspondence they are often warned that it would be 'inadvisable' for them to continue. And as always, no foreign newspapers can be bought in Russia except communist ones.

There are wise men of the new generation working behind the scenes to enlarge liberty in particular contexts, and they sometimes succeed. But there are others who profit by the clumsy old set-up, or who are genuinely afraid of what might happen if the brakes were taken off. The reformers are hampered by the weight of Russian attitudes as well as by Party control; often it is the Party which is in advance of tradition.

The Government must by now feel pretty sure of the strength of popular support for the system, and we should not be surprised at further relaxations. But the Government's attitude will remain ambivalent for several reasons:

(1) Because the U.S.S.R. is still backward in so many respects, and still needs to train very large numbers of people to get rid of the backwardness and to want to do so.

(2) Because even if there were enough of such persons,

the Government would not feel they could trust the free-ranging individual as we do in Western countries. This is partly because they are Communists and partly because they are Russians.

(3) They believe that Communism must eventually come to power all over the world, but though they may help other countries to Communism, they are not going to run the slightest risk of weakening the Soviet Union in doing so. The continued progress and increasing power of the U.S.S.R. come before international Communism, where a choice has to be made between the two, and so foreign influence and contacts with foreigners must be severely restricted, in case another way of life should seduce Soviet citizens. As the Soviet standard of living rises, and provided that the threat of war recedes, more freedom will probably be allowed to foreign contacts.

(4) Finally, the Soviet leaders fear the menaces of war and the violence of anti-Communist feeling in many circles in the United States and other countries.

It was the Soviet Government under Stalin which started the Cold War, to the disappointment of the world, at a time when the U.S.S.R. had the goodwill of the majority of world opinion on account of her wartime victories and sufferings. The Cold War was probably started in order to keep out foreign influences—Communists don't need the goodwill of bourgeois—and to keep at arm's length anyone who might nose out the weakness of the U.S.S.R. in the years immediately after the war. By this policy, of course, the Soviet Government added many rows of dragon's teeth to those which they had already sown.

Today Mr. Khrushchev says war between Communist and capitalist countries is not inevitable, and he has taken a good many steps in the endeavour to show that they can live alongside each other. His foreign propaganda is nowadays not much aimed at the prosperous, industrialized West, but at the peasant populations of Asia and Africa. If one of these backward countries seems ready to drop like a ripe plum into the Communist grasp it will not be rejected. But if the Western powers have made clear beforehand that such an addition to world Communist power would be regarded as a matter for world war, the plum will not be ripe, and it will not be grasped. The tension between the two sides is only going to relax very, very slowly; threat will be answered by threat, and stonewalling by stonewalling, for a long time to come, though the danger of world nuclear war is now realized by a sufficient number of the leaders—if not all the leaders— on both sides, and that realization seems likely to condition their actions if not always their language.

This book is meant to give an idea of the state of things in the Soviet Union, and not to be a study of international relations, which would deserve another book in themselves. The international situation might be better understood, however, if less attention were sometimes paid to 'the clash of ideologies' or the stalemates at conferences, and more to the internal situation of the countries concerned. Most of the Western countries have moved far away from the kind of 'capitalism' pictured by Marx, and the U.S.S.R. now presents a very different picture from the simple, crude image of 'Communism' which is too often accepted in the West. For one thing, the crude Marxist interpretations in social matters, in the arts, and even in international matters are now modified by more realistic attitudes. Simple economic relations are not invoked to explain everything, and a great deal of reliable information about foreign countries now reaches Soviet governing circles, who must often be far more accurately informed about the outside world than Stalin ever was.

We can now also see that the U.S.S.R. remains an old-fashioned society in comparison with most countries in the West. Its standards are measured by ideal models rather than average models, with one result which many Westerners might find desirable, in the rather high moral tone—the complete absence of pornography, for example —which prevails in Soviet institutions and among most Soviet people. Other Westerners might object, however, that the Soviet attitude arises more from prohibition than from self-discipline, and that it slurs over some of the facts about human nature. For in the West—mainly under the influence of the recent rich development of the social and psychological sciences—we are busy adapting our institutions and our atmosphere to the measure of the average imperfect man, woman, or child. But in the U.S.S.R. these sciences are still mostly held down by Marxist and traditional Russian attitudes. There is plenty of good-will exerted for the benefit of the people, but a great reluctance to study human nature closely in the mean.

However, the U.S.S.R. seems to be coming to a greater development of the individual, and even of individualism, and this is coming about through industrialization under socialism. The Western peoples, on the other hand, have had a very powerful development of individualism for many centuries, generated originally perhaps by the Western Churches, and fostered by the 'bourgeois' institutions of individual farming and private industrial enterprise. If the Russians become more individualistic their socialism will not thereby be invalidated, and their concept of 'the individual' will continue to be different from ours. And, if as seems likely, many of the Western countries become more socialist in their institutions, the individualism which built up so much of their prosperity will not be invalidated either, and their socialism will naturally look different from the Soviet version.

# SUGGESTIONS FOR FURTHER READING

*1. Pictures:* Few people visit Russia, and newspapers print few photographs of Russian subjects; it seems even more important with Russia than with other countries to look at a great many photographs so as to get some idea of the country and the people:

A. HOWARD & E. NEWMAN, *Pictorial History of Russia* (Hutchinson, 1943).

H. CARTIER-BRESSON, *The People of Moscow* (Thames & Hudson, 1955). A little out of date as to clothing, but pictures are by one of the world's greatest 'intimate' photographers.

*Russia in Pictures; from Moscow to Samarkand.* (Duckworth, 1956).

M. HÜRLIMANN, *Moscow and Leningrad* (Thames & Hudson, 1958).

C. W. THAYER & the editors of *Life, Russia (Sunday Times,* 1961). Useful introductory text also.

*2. General:*

G. GORER & J. RICKMAN, *The People of Great Russia: a psychological study* (Cresset Press, 1949).

JOHN GUNTHER, *Inside Russia Today* (Hamish Hamilton, 1958).

WRIGHT MILLER, *Russians as People* (Phoenix House, 1960).

T. FITZSIMMONS & others, *U.S.S.R.* (Mayflower, 1961). The most comprehensive and reliable book yet published about the Soviet Union, yet not merely a work of reference; it can be read straight through.

S. V. UTECHIN & others, *Everyman's Concise Encyclopædia of Russia* (Dent, 1961).

*3. Geography:*

T. SHABAD, *Geography of the U.S.S.R.: a regional survey* (O.U.P., 1951).

COLE & GERMAN, *Geography of the U.S.S.R.* (Butterworth, 1961). The most up-to-date.

G. JORRÉ, *The Soviet Union: the land and its people* (Longmans, 1961).

*4. History:*

J. W. LAWRENCE, *Russia in the Making* (Allen & Unwin, 1957). Gives a good outline of 'what one needs to know before visiting Russia'.

B. H. SUMNER, *Survey of Russian History* (Duckworth, 1961 reprinted). A superb study of Russian history under headings, e.g. 'The Law', 'The Church'.

Excellent and very readable histories, tracing the influences that have made modern Russia, are those by A. Mazour, *Russia Past & Present* (Van Nostrand, 1957), Melvin Wren, *The Course of Russian History* (Macmillan of New York, 1958), and Warren B. Walsh, *Russia and the Soviet Union* (Cresset Press for Michigan University Press, 1959).

*5. Religion:* Whatever one's feelings about religion, it is most important to read about the religion of the Russians; to do so may also give one a fresh idea of what religion can be.

N. BERDYAEV, *The Origins of Russian Communism* (Bles, 1937). A distinguished theological writer examines Communist roots in the Russian Church and Russian traditions.

N. ZERNOV, *The Russians and Their Church* (Hutchinson, 1945). Actually a simple and most readable history of the Russian People.

G. FEDOTOV, *The Russian Religious Mind* (O.U.P. for Harvard University Press, 1946).

WALTER KOLARZ, *Religion in the Soviet Union* (Macmillan, 1961).

*6. The Revolution:*

SIR R. BRUCE LOCKHART, *The Two Revolutions: an eye-witness study* (Phoenix House, 1957).

ALAN MOOREHEAD, *The Russian Revolution* (Collins & Hamish Hamilton, 1958).

### 7. *The Stalin Period—Collectivization, Five-Year Plans, & the Terror:*

MAURICE HINDUS, *Red Bread* (Cape, 1931). A warm and first-hand account of collective farming by a Russian-born correspondent.

W. H. CHAMBERLAIN, *Russia's Iron Age* (Duckworth, 1935). A vivid account of the years 1930-35.

ISAAC DEUTSCHER, *Stalin: a political biography* (O.U.P., 1949).

F. BECK & W. GODIN, *Russian Purge and the Extraction of Confession* (Hurst & Blackett, 1951). A most objective and useful short book by two who suffered.

W. RESWICK, *I Dreamt Revolution* (Regnery, Chicago, 1952). A Russian-born correspondent who was a friend of the purged leaders tells how Stalin destroyed opposition.

V. & E. PETROV, *Empire of Fear* (Deutsch, 1956). A husband and wife who fled from the Soviet Secret Service give a warm impression of much of Soviet life.

### 8. *The Khrushchev Period:*

EDWARD CRANKSHAW, *Khrushchev's Russia* (Penguin, 1959).

HARRISON SALISBURY, *To Moscow—and Beyond* (Michael Joseph, 1960).

ALEXANDER WERTH, *The Khrushchev Phase* (Hale, 1961). The most intimate of these three.

### 9. *Marxism:*

J. PLAMENATZ, *What is Communism?* (National News-Letter, 1947). Short and most useful.

SIDNEY HOOK, *Marx and the Marxists: the ambiguous legacy* (Van Nostrand, Anvil Books, 1955). Treats of both theory and practice, and includes extracts from important texts.

S. HENDEL (ed.), *The Soviet Crucible: Soviet government in theory & practice* (Van Nostrand, 1959). An anthology of Marxist writings and criticisms of Marxism and of the Soviet system.

*10. Government and Economic Systems:*

BARRINGTON MOORE, *Soviet Politics: The Dilemma of Power* (O.U.P. for Harvard University Press, 1950). Tries to explain how decisions are actually taken in the U.S.S.R.

J. N. HAZARD, *The Soviet System of Government* (C.U.P. for Chicago University Press, 1960).

*The Soviet Seven Year Plan* (Phoenix House, 1960). A short but excellent account of the state and prospects of the Soviet economy.

R. W. CAMPBELL, *Soviet Economic Power* (Stevens for Houghton Mifflin, 1960). A very good introduction which needs no economic training on the part of the reader.

Those who know something of economics should look at—

N. JASNY, *The Soviet 1956 Statistical Handbook* (Michigan State University Press, 1957), and

ALEC NOVE, *The Soviet Economy* (Allen & Unwin, 1961).

*11. Education, the Arts, and Science:*

*Education in the U.S.S.R.* (U.S. Department of Health, Education & Welfare, 1957). (Obtainable from H.M. Stationery Office.) A very good introduction.

G. L. KLINE (ed.), *Soviet Education* (Routledge, 1957). Essays by Soviet refugee teachers or students.

MARK FIELD, *Doctor and Patient in Soviet Russia* (O.U.P. for Harvard University Press, 1958).

FAUBION BOWERS, *Entertainment in Russia* (Nelson, 1959). A wide survey based on personal experience.

GEORGE GIBIAN, *Interval of Freedom: Soviet literature during the 'thaw' of 1954-57* (O.U.P. for University of Minnesota Press, 1960). Gives a good idea of the general atmosphere of the period.

JAY LEYDA, *Kino; a history of the Russian and Soviet film* (Allen & Unwin, 1960). A large and important book by an American who spent three years in Soviet film studios and film schools.

HELENE BELLEW, *Ballet in Moscow Today* (Thames & Hudson, 1956).

G. Hamilton, *The Art and Architecture of Russia* (Penguin, 1954). A standard work, part of the Pelican History of Art.

*12. More Imaginative Works, and Fiction:*

To get a feeling of the Russian people one should read at least, among classical Russian novels, Tolstoy's *Anna Karenina.*

Some Soviet novels bring a great deal of the contemporary scene to life:

Nicholas Ostrovsky, *How the Steel was Tempered* (Foreign Languages Publishing House, Moscow). The classic novel about the Civil War by a young working man who took part in it.

Alexei Tolstoy, *The Road to Calvary* (Hutchinson, 1945). A rather untidy novel about the Revolution and Civil War, which stresses miseries more than enthusiasms.

I. Ilf and E. Petrov, *The Little Golden Calf* (Grayson) and *Diamonds to Sit On* (also called *Twelve Chairs*) (Methuen, 1930). Are comic Soviet classics of the earlier chaotic years.

M. Sholokhov, *Virgin Soil Upturned* (Putnam, 1935) and *And Quiet Flows the Don* (Putnam, 1957, and Four-Square Books). Give a robust picture of Cossack life during the collectivization and during the civil war respectively.

A. Makarenko, *The Road to Life* (Foreign Languages Publishing House, Moscow). Is not a novel but the true story of a delinquent colony led by the remarkable educator Makarenko, whose attitudes and methods are still standard in Russia.

Mikhail Prishvin, *The Black Arab and other stories* (Hutchinson, 1947). A beautiful writer on nature and country life.

Mikhail Zoshchenko, *The Wonderful Dog and other stories* (Methuen, 1942) and *The Women Who Couldn't Read and other stories* (Methuen, 1940). Very short stories with an artless irony which is typically Russian.

Boris Pasternak, *Dr. Zhivago* (Collins, 1958, and Fontana Books). Gives a most poetic impression of Russian humanity, sensibility, and country life, but no reflection of the enthusiasms which helped to build modern Russia.

VLADIMIR DUDINTSEV, *Not by Bread Alone* (Hutchinson 1957). Throws light on a great many of the newer attitudes.

Among imaginatively-written works, or semi-fiction, which help to give a vivid impression:

H. TROYAT, *Daily Life in Russia under the Last Tsar* (Allen & Unwin, 1961).

S. GOUZENKO, *Before Igor—memories of a Soviet Youth* (Cassell, 1961). A most lively evocation of earlier Soviet days, by an apparently unembittered refugee.

WRIGHT MILLER, *Young Traveller in Russia* (Phoenix House, 1958).

Firsthand accounts by visitors or journalists have a liveliness which other books rarely possess, but unfortunately they soon become out of date. Very enjoyable, and still reliable pictures of their period, are:

SIR R. BRUCE LOCKHART, *Memoirs of a Secret Agent* (Putnam, 1932). Includes an eyewitness account of the Revolution; so does the story of another secret agent:

SIR PAUL DUKES, *ST 25* (Cassell, 1938).

L. C. STEVENS, *Life in Russia* (Longmans, 1954). A long and intimate account of his experiences during 1947-49 by the U.S. Naval Attaché

SALLY BELFRAGE, *A Room in Moscow* (Deutsch, 1958). Light-hearted and unexaggerated.

SANTHA RAMA RAU, *My Russian Journey* (Gollancz, 1959). Three months in 1957 described modestly and naturally by an Indian lady.

I. R. LEVINE, *The Real Russia* (W. H. Allen, 1959). First hand impression of ten years by an American correspondent who frequently contributed to the London *Times*.

# SOME DATES IN RUSSIAN HISTORY

about 300 onwards    Armenia and Georgia Christianized

[432 onwards    Ireland and then Scotland Christianized]

[596 onwards    (St. Augustine). England Christianized]

860    First expedition of Varangians against Constantinople

[870    King Alfred crowned]

988    *Vladimir* of Kiev and his people became Christian

1147    First written mention of Moscow

[1166 onwards    Growth of national system of law in England]

1237-42    Mongol conquest of Russia

1252-63    *Alexander Nevsky*, grand prince of Vladimir

[1265 onwards    Beginnings of English Parliament]

1325-41    *Ivan I* of Moscow ('Kalita' or 'Moneybags')

1367-81    Kremlin first fortified in stone

1380    Battle of Kulikovo: Tartars defeated by Dmitri Donskoy

[1381    Peasants' Revolt in England. Serfdom fades away]

1453    Turks capture Constantinople

1462-1505    *Ivan III, The Great*—first Tsar

[1476    Caxton begins printing in London]

1480    Mongol rule ended

1533-84    *Ivan IV, The Terrible*

[1534 onwards    Church of England breaks away from Rome]

about 1550    Military service established on basis of land tenure

1552    Kazan (Tartar capital) captured; St. Basil's Cathedral built in celebration

1553   Chancellor opens White Sea route from Britain to Russia

1564   First book printed in Moscow

1571   Crimean Tartars burn Moscow

about 1570-1600   Cossack settlements begin on the 'frontier'

1581   Yermak leads conquest of Siberia

1598-1605   *Boris Godunov*

1610-12   Poles in Moscow

1613-45   *Michael Romanov*

1640   Russians reach the Pacific

1649   Last vestige of escape for serfs removed

[1649   Charles I of England executed]

1654 onwards   Great Schism in the Russian Church

1654   Ukraine united with Russia

1670-1   Peasant revolt led by Stenka Razin

1682-1725   *Peter the Great*

1697-8   Peter visits Western countries

1703   St. Petersburg (Leningrad) founded

1709   Peter defeats Swedes at Poltava

1721   Treaty of Nystad confirms Peter's conquests from Sweden

1725   Academy of Sciences founded

1755   Moscow University founded

1756-63   Seven Years' War

1762-96   *Catherine the Great*

1772   First Partition of Poland

1774   Black Sea steppes conquered from Turkey

1773-5   Peasant revolt under Pugachov

1780   Armed Neutrality against England

1783   Crimea incorporated in Russia

[1789   French Revolution]

1793   Second Partition of Poland

1795   Third (complete) Partition of Poland

1801-25   *Alexander I*

# SOME DATES IN RUSSIAN HISTORY

1801-29  Conquest of Transcaucasia

1812  Great Fatherland War against Napoleon

1814-15  Congress of Vienna

1825-55  *Nicholas I*

1825  Decembrist rising

1830-1  Polish rebellion suppressed

1853-56  Crimean War against Turkey, Britain, and France

1855-81  *Alexander II*

1855-60  Far Eastern provinces acquired from China

1861  Emancipation of the serfs

1863  Polish Rebellion suppressed

1863-4  Independent courts established, with trial by jury. Some state schools founded. Local councils (*zemstva*) began

1864-85  Central Asian provinces conquered

1867  Alaska sold to the United States

1881-94  *Alexander III*

1885-87  Famine

1891  Trans-Siberian railway begun

1894-1917  *Nicholas II*

1900  Manchuria occupied

1904-5  Russo-Japanese War

1905  'The First Revolution'

1906  First Duma

1906-11  Land reforms of Stolypin

1914  First World War begins

1917  March Revolution
November (Bolshevik) Revolution

1918  Treaty of Brest-Litovsk

1918-20  Civil War and War of Intervention

1921-2  Famine

1921-8  Period of New Economic Policy

1924  Lenin died

1927  Trotsky expelled. Stalin in power

1928-32    First Five Year Plan; agriculture collectivized
1933-37    Second Five Year Plan
[1933    Nazi Revolution in Germany]
1934    U.S.S.R. admitted to League of Nations
1935    Soviet-French alliance signed
[1936-9    Spanish Civil War]
[1938    Czechoslovakia handed over to Germany at Munich]
1939    August: Soviet-German alliance signed
September: Second World War began. U.S.S.R. occupied Eastern Poland, Estonia, Latvia, and Lithuania
1939-40    Soviet-Finnish War. U.S.S.R. expelled from League of Nations
1941    Germany invaded U.S.S.R.
1945    End of World War
1946-51    Fourth Five Year Plan
1953    Stalin died
1956    Twentieth Party Congress; Khrushchev attacks Stalin
1961    New Programme of Communist Party of the U.S.S.R.
1959-65    Seven Year Plan

# INDEX

# INDEX

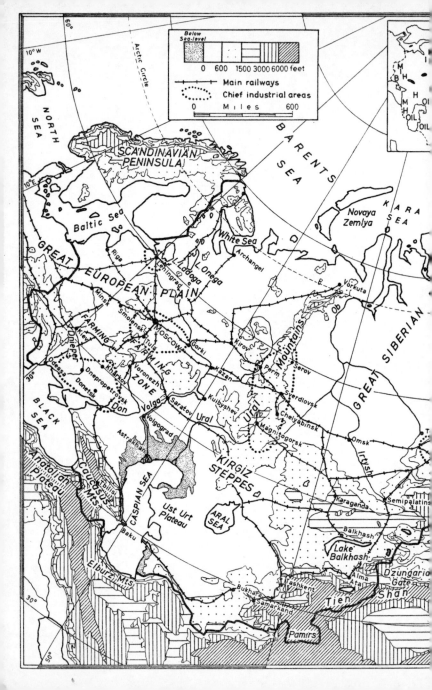